THE HIGH HIMALAYA

Published by
The Mountaineers Books
1001 SW Klickitat Way, Suite 201
Seattle, WA 98134

First edition, 2001

No part of this book may be reproduced in
any form, or by any electronic, mechanical,
or other means, without permission in
writing from the publisher.

Published simultaneously in Great Britain by
Cordee, 3a DeMontfort Street, Leicester,
England, LE1 7HD

Manufactured in Hong Kong

Acquiring Editor: David Emblidge
Project Editor: Kathleen Cubley
Copy Editor: Kris Fulsaas
Design and layout: Ani Rucki
Cartographer: Tony Moore
Source Map: Mountain High Maps® ©1993
  Digital Wisdom Inc.
Digital Production and Scanning, Getty
  Images/Seattle: Richelle Barnes, Matthew
  Flor, Jason Wiley, Lou Kings, Johnny
  Hubbard, Stacey Lester, Curt Waller, Tim
  Perciful, Jay Sakamato
Image Management and Digital Prepress,
  Art Wolfe, Inc.: Gilbert Neri
Project Editor, Wildlands Press: Ray Pfortner
Photo and Text Editors, Art Wolfe, Inc.:
  Deirdre Skillman, Gavriel Jecan
Project Planners, Art Wolfe, Inc.: Christine
  Eckhoff, Lisa Woods
Product Development, Wildlands Press:
  Craig Scheak, Kate Campbell

All photographs © Art Wolfe unless
otherwise noted

Cover photograph: *Ultar Peak (24,240 feet/
7,388 meters), Hunza Valley, Pakistan*

Frontispiece: *Star trails over Mount Everest
(29,035 feet/8,850 meters), Nepal*

Library of Congress Cataloging-in-Publication Data
Wolfe, Art.
    The high Himalaya / Art Wolfe ; Peter
  Potterfield in conversation with Reinhold
  Messner, Doug Scott, Ed Viesturs—1st ed.
      p. cm.
Includes bibliographical references (p.) and
index.
    ISBN 0-89886-841-6 (hard cover)
    1. Mountaineering—Himalaya
  Mountains. 2. Mountaineers—Interviews.
  3. Messner, Reinhold, 1944—Interviews.
  4. Scott, Doug K.—Interviews.
  5. Viesturs, Ed.—Interviews. 6. Himalaya
  Mountains—Description and travel.
  I. Potterfield, Peter. II. Title.
GV199.44.H55 W65 2001
796.52'2'095496—dc21
                    2001002405

THE HIGH

HIMALAYA

ART WOLFE

PETER POTTERFIELD IN CONVERSATION WITH

- REINHOLD MESSNER
- DOUG SCOTT
- ED VIESTURS

FOREWORD BY NORBU TENZING NORGAY

THE MOUNTAINEERS BOOKS ■ WILDLANDS PRESS

CONTENTS

DEDICATION

I would like to dedicate this book
to the climbers who invited me
on an incredible Mount Everest
expedition, and to the friends
who shared the experience.

The 1984 Ultima Thule
Expedition Participants:

Gene Bauer

Bob Berg

Ben Blackett

Tom Clement

Mike Colpitts

Tom Fitzsimmons

Rick Foutch

Jim Frush

Don Goodman

Dave Hambly

Kurt Hanson

Phil Hawkins

Anton Karuza

Ray Nichols

Warren Thompson

Greg Thompson

Mal Stamper

Keren Su

Mike Weidman

Rich Wohns

Evans Wyckoff

John Yaeger

And, to my friends who lost their
lives pursuing their personal dreams
and lofty goals:

Glenn Brindeiro

Agris Moruss

Scott Fischer

A.W.

NORBU TENZING NORGAY

Fifty years ago, the Himalaya became known to the world. But it has always been there.

When I think back to 1953, to Edmund Hillary and my father, Tenzing Norgay, on Mount Everest, I realize their ascent signified that the mountain belonged not to one nation but to everyone. There couldn't have been two better people to be first on the summit. They have exemplified what climbing is about: respectful collaboration toward a shared goal. But what many don't know is that their biggest challenges came when they went back to the Himalaya, not to climb mountains but to help the people who live there.

Photo © Iwona Boretti

If we believe that the mountains belong to all of us, then we are all responsible for them. In the past, traveling in the Himalaya was strictly for trekkers and die-hard mountain enthusiasts, or those wealthy enough to go. That is no longer the case. These days, record numbers of people from all over the world are going there. That is good, for I believe, as my father did, that travel is the best form of education and communication. It fosters international friendship and understanding, and many deep ties are formed on these trips.

But tourism has its impact, environmentally, socially, culturally, and economically. Commonly it is signified by the number of teahouses in the Khumbu or the increased number of people and houses in Kathmandu. These changes are inevitable, and we must accept them as a fact of life. The challenge we face is to bring positive changes, changes that the locals believe in. Then there is not only change, there is progress.

Many people have benefited from the increased tourism in the mountains, but many have not. People of the Himalaya still struggle to survive, they still live day to day, and often there is little economic security. The ones in need, however, are often not the ones who are the beneficiaries.

That's why projects like this book can be helpful. Art Wolfe's stunning images capture the beauty and hardship of the people living on the roof of the world. Author Peter Potterfield's recent work on the Internet attests to the interest in the Himalaya that prevails all over the world. The perspectives of Reinhold Messner, Doug Scott, and Ed Viesturs that Potterfield brings to us are invaluable to those who care about the Himalayan region because they come from long associations and experience. These are men of the mountains, and they show how high the level of friendship, commitment, and communication—despite language barriers—can go. They genuinely care about giving something back to the people and places they have received so much from.

Giving back, then, is the key. Those of us who have been there know the powerful influence exerted by the mountains, and this personal adventure motivates us to do something positive in return. I think what we need to understand is that when we give, we should give with a genuine heart, without expectations of return or to own something, but simply to give because of the friends we have made or the experiences we have had.

There are many ways to give back. I think every form

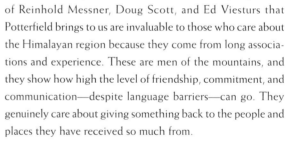

◀ Thamserkhu (21,279 feet/6,623 meters), Khumbu region ⌁ Nepal

◀◀ Predawn light, Concordia, Karakoram Range ⌁ Pakistan

of communication, whether a book such as this one, a movie, or a slide show, can help in raising funds. So my message is to give, yes, but to do so responsibly. See where the real needs are, make sure there is community involvement, make sure that what you give to is something that will be well taken care of. The ultimate goal is to contribute toward self-sufficiency and sustainability, with sensitivity toward cultural identity.

It's often more productive to give through the good organizations that work in the Himalaya. But the world of nonprofit organizations is not perfect either, so people should ensure that what they give will go to the people in need. They should understand who they are giving to, and understand how their gift will be spent. In that way, everyone can benefit.

The Himalaya are vast, reaching into many countries, including Tibet, Nepal, India, Bhutan, and Pakistan. Although many people in those places have benefited from the efforts of friends such as Ed Hillary and organizations such as the American Himalayan Foundation, there is still a vast number of people who continue to struggle each day whether they are Tibetans, Sherpas, Nepalis, or Lobas. Much has been done, but a lot more can and needs to be done.

My grandfather lived to be ninety years old in the village of Thame, living off the land, herding yaks, and trading with Tibetans. He benefited not at all from tourism. The same is true today: There are people who remain on the periphery, and often those are the people most in need. How do you go about finding them? How do you go about helping them?

There is no simple answer, and that is why those of us who care must give responsibly. As more and more people visit the Himalaya, more will come home motivated to help. This presents vast possibilities for positive change for the people of the mountains.

I never felt any pressure from my father to do this kind of work on behalf of the people of the Himalaya. I came to it by accident, after a career in the travel business, and feel lucky to find work consistent with my personal beliefs. My father emphasized to my siblings and me, from a very young age, the greatness of humility. I understand now that it is impossible to achieve everything I want to in a single lifetime. I can only work hard, work carefully, and do as much as I can. It's all about karma. In essence, our humanity is judged by our compassion.

Norbu Tenzing Norgay
Director of Development
American Himalayan Foundation
San Francisco

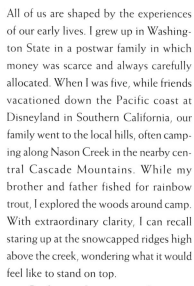

INTRODUCTION
ART WOLFE

All of us are shaped by the experiences of our early lives. I grew up in Washington State in a postwar family in which money was scarce and always carefully allocated. When I was five, while friends vacationed down the Pacific coast at Disneyland in Southern California, our family went to the local hills, often camping along Nason Creek in the nearby central Cascade Mountains. While my brother and father fished for rainbow trout, I explored the woods around camp. With extraordinary clarity, I can recall staring up at the snowcapped ridges high above the creek, wondering what it would feel like to stand on top.

By the time I was sixteen, I was poring over topographic maps of Washington's Olympic and Cascade Mountains. In 1970, I enrolled at the University of Washington in Seattle as an art major. I also enrolled in a basic mountaineering class. During the week, I learned the rules of composition and design. On the weekends, I learned the rudimentary skills of climbing. By the time I finished the climbing class, I had the skills needed to go beyond the heather-clad lower slopes and reach the glacier-sculpted summits. As my new acquaintances sought climbing companions, I became immersed in the world of climbing.

In 1971, my parents gave me a used Konica camera for Christmas. I always took it with me to document my mountain adventures. I began giving slide presentations to less intrepid friends back home, sharing my experiences. Photog-

raphy soon became the tail that wagged the dog. Now I began to select climbs for their photographic potential rather than their physical challenge. Applying the lessons learned in art class to my mountain photographs, I did not realize at the time that a career shift had undeniably occurred.

By the mid-1970s, I began carrying a 4x5 (large-format) view camera to take black-and-white panoramas from the summits. In 1977, after graduating from college, I sold my first photographs—four 8-foot-square wall murals of—what else?—the North Cascades to—whom else?—the North Face climbing store in Seattle.

In November 1980, I accompanied three friends to Tanzania in Africa, where we climbed Mount Kilimanjaro, my first international climbing experience. Two years later, one of those friends, Glen Brindero, introduced me to a Seattle climbing team planning an expedition to Mount Everest. Glen was one of the cornerstones of this team, and with his lobbying, I was invited to come along as the expedition's photographer. The expedition was called the Ultima Thule Everest Expedition. Loosely translated from Greek, *Ultima Thule* means "the edge of the Earth, corner of the sky." We would be the first Western climbing team permitted by China to attempt the famed and little-known Northeast Ridge route through Tibet since British climbers George Mallory and Andrew Irvine disappeared on it in 1924.

◀ Lingtren (22,027 feet/6,714 meters) ᴖ— Tibet

▲ Art Wolfe, Baltoro Glacier ᴖ— Pakistan

▶ West Face, Mount Everest, Himalaya Range ᴖ— Nepal

▶▶ Blanket flowers *(Gaillardia spp.)*, Indus River Valley, Skardu ᴖ— Pakistan

Tragically, Glen perished in an avalanche while climbing Pakistan's Gasherbrum II in 1982. Though badly shaken by the loss, I stayed with the expedition. On March 27, 1984, the day of the Lunar New Year celebration, we arrived in Lhasa, Tibet. Few Westerners were allowed into Tibet prior to 1984, so when we arrived wearing our bright red parkas, a near riot erupted as we were mobbed by curious Tibetans, many of whom had just completed their own pilgrimages to Lhasa to visit the holiest of Buddhist monasteries, the Potala Palace. I will never forget the scene as we toured the Potala with its labyrinthine passageways, candlelit and packed with thousands of Tibetan herders. At times, the Tibetans were more interested in us than in the holy temple they had traveled so far to see.

From Lhasa we traveled through increasingly remote villages and finally to the base camp of Everest at 17,000 feet. For nearly three months our team tried to get a man on the summit, but eventually we ran out of time. Two of our climbers nearly summitted, failing by a mere 800 feet. Bad weather, illness, and the departure of high-altitude porters created inescapable delays. According to our Chinese climbing permit, we had to be off the mountain and out of China by June 5 or face a $50,000 penalty. With neither the resources nor time, we had no choice but to leave. Of the thirteen expeditions attempting Everest that spring, we were the only team to avoid severe injury or loss of life. The physicians on our expedition advanced the knowledge of the treatment of high-altitude cerebral edema. And in the end, we all could say we participated in a grand adventure for three months among the highest, most spectacular mountains on Earth.

The experiences of the Ultima Thule expedition compelled me to travel again and again in the Himalaya. Several years later, I traveled to Nepal, where I followed the main route to Everest from Lukla, up the Khumbu Valley from the south. These south slopes are a sharp contrast to the much drier, less vegetated, high, flat Tibetan Plateau, punctuated as they are by steeply cut river canyons and enchanted forests of rhododendrons, birches, and pines all covered with lichens, sedges, and mosses.

One of my most memorable trips to the high Himalaya occurred in August 1996, when I traveled to Pakistan, into the Skardu Valley along the Indus River. For three weeks we followed the river valley, ascending onto the Baltoro Glacier, which provides access to the greatest range in the Himalaya— the Karakoram. The glacier serves as a frozen highway into the inner mountains; without it the mountains would be almost inaccessible. The Baltoro was our roadway and our home. At night we would pitch our tents on the glacier and fall asleep to the groans of cracking ice hundreds of feet below us.

I can see why photographers, trekkers, and climbers love the high Himalaya. It is certainly not just the physical challenge of these mountains. Practically every bend in the trail and crest of the ridge reveals a stunning vista that literally takes your breath away. This place is unique in all the world. Nature dominates here as no other place that I have ever been. It is simply overwhelming. One cannot come here and not feel a reverence for the natural world—not just for animate life but also the inanimate, for rock and soil, ice and snow. Nowhere else on Earth is one so dwarfed by the scale of things, so aware of mankind's place in the larger scheme of things.

Every time I stand among the high Himalaya, in awe and reverence, I redouble my resolve to showcase through my work the grandeur that is nature, to emphasize humanity's place and humanity's responsibility to work with nature and for nature, to try to make a difference. We all have a responsibility to help ensure that as many of the Earth's remaining wild places as possible stay that way. The high Himalaya remind us of all that is at stake.

▲▲ Detail of a hand, Kathmandu ✦— Nepal
▲ Decorative beads, Bouddhanath Stupa, Kathmandu ✦— Nepal

◄ Mother and child, Kathmandu ✦— Nepal
▶ Everest expedition members in front of the North Face of Mount Everest ✦— Tibet

ON THE HIMALAYA

PETER POTTERFIELD

Photo © James Martin

The Himalaya is the youngest, highest, and most complex region of mountains on Earth. Stretching for almost two thousand miles (3,200 kilometers) from one end of Central Asia to the other, the range forms a vast arc of towering peaks, converging subranges, and massive drainages. This is the place where the Indian subcontinent crashed into Asia in a cataclysmic plate-tectonic event that hasn't stopped yet. Along this arc, the crushed and twisted mantle of the Earth has risen up to create a mountain barrier of such moment that it has defined cultural differences, religious movements, and political boundaries for centuries. The component subranges, plateaus, and drainages of the epic swath of peaks are so big and so diverse that just trying to comprehend them as a single range is daunting.

The peaks, subranges, and river valleys that comprise the Himalaya were created by the same monumental collision of tectonic plates, but with weird aberrations. Although scientists agree that the range is the result of the Indian Plate sliding under the Asian landmass, there's a place in the western Karakoram, at Chalt, where the Indian subcontinent is riding up over Asia to expose a seabed of odd greenish rock millions of years old. In the Himalaya generalizations are problematic.

"We know for a fact that the range is moving northward," says Bradford Washburn, the preeminent mountain geologist from Boston's Museum of Science, "at about the same rate that your fingernails grow. And I'm convinced that the Himalaya is growing, but it is growing by fits and starts, which means you have periods of quiet when no measurable movement takes place."

Even as the inexorable forces of its creation continue, the Himalayan Range remains unusual in that it has no natural climax, no gradual buildup to a single giant massif. It is, instead, a mind-boggling spine of mountains in distinct subranges that stretch from the Indus River in northern Pakistan to the Brahmaputra River in northeastern India and beyond. The highest point in the range, 29,035-foot (8,850-meter) Mount Everest (named in 1859 for Sir George Everest, Britain's surveyor general of India during its colonization), is near the eastern end of the range, on the Nepal-Tibet border. The second tallest of these mountains, 28,250-foot (8,611-meter) K2 (so named in 1856 because it was the second peak in the Karakoram Range surveyed by the British), lies 800 miles (about 1,280 kilometers) away near the western end of the great arc, in Pakistan near its border with China.

But even these two giants don't in fact embrace the entire range. The absolute western end of this mighty crescent of mountains is marked by the Pamirs, a subrange where the borders of Tajikistan, Afghanistan, and China intersect, dominated by 24,590-foot (7,482-meter) Communism Peak. The peaks marking the extreme eastern flank of the range are the obscure mountains on the border between Tibet and the Indian state of Assam, dominated by 25,445-foot (7,756-meter) Namcha Barwa. Some outriders lie farther east still, in China, including peaks such as 24,790-foot (7,556-meter) Minya Konka. In between these extreme outposts is a chaos of high

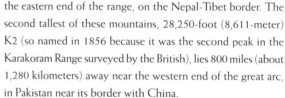

▲ Panorama including Pumo-Ri (23,198 feet/7,145 meters), Rongbuk Glacier ∾ Tibet

◀ Chang-tzu (24,770 feet/7,550 meters) above Cho La Pass ∾ China mountains strung out with hardly a break, including a couple of freestanding anomalies such as 26,660-foot (8,126-meter) Nanga Parbat, whose very name means "naked mountain," reflecting the fact it stands apart from the other peaks.

The geographic highlights of the Himalaya clearly are the Karakoram Range of Pakistan and the Nepal Himalaya of Nepal and Tibet. Within these two subranges lie all fourteen of the world's 8,000-meter peaks—those rare mountains taller than 26,240 feet. But from the Pamirs (and its neighboring ranges, the Tien Shan and Hindu Kush) in the west to the Assam Himalaya and Minya Konka in the east, the range includes at least *four hundred* peaks over 7,000 meters, and many more higher than 6,000 meters. From the major drainages— the Indus, Sutlej, Brahmaputra, and Ganges River systems— comes much of the water that flows across Asia and India. Taken together, this mountain landscape is unlike any other on the planet in scale and size, and it is populated with peoples of equally diverse cultures, religions, and political orientation.

In Nepal alone, there are thirty-six ethnic subgroups or tribes that live in the mountains of the tiny kingdom. The Sherpa are probably the best known of all Himalayan people by virtue of their close and early connections with Westerners who came to climb the mountains, notably Everest. But many of the people referred to as "Sherpa" because they work in the trekking industry are in fact Tamang, Garung, Chettri, Rai, or other tribes, each with a different language and culture. The Sherpa, Tamang, Thakali, and other Nepalese peoples share Mongol features and speak a Tibeto-Burmese– based language; the Brahmin, Chettri, and other Nepalese ethnic groups originating from farther south speak languages derived from India. Buddhism is practiced throughout the eastern Himalaya; Hinduism is prevalent in the lowlands.

Near the other great cluster of high peaks, the Karakoram in Pakistan, cultural origins are equally complex. At least eighty-four major ethnic groups have been identified. The Balti people, perhaps the best known among the Pakistani mountain peoples because of their exposure to Western climb-

ers and trekkers in the Baltoro Glacier region, actually arrived from Tibet in waves between six hundred to eight hundred years ago. Originally Buddhists, the Baltis converted to Islam in the late 1500s, but their language remains based on ancient Tibetan. Islam prevails throughout the western Himalaya. Near Nanga Parbat the Kohistani, sometimes called Diamiri, are a fiercely independent people who even today remain semi-autonomous. In the eastern Hushe Valley of Pakistan, another area of high peaks, the people are a mix of Balti and Kashmiri; farther north, up beyond Gilgit toward Rakaposhi, the people are Burushashki. Urdu is the lingua franca of Pakistan, allowing these diverse people a means of communication, much as Nepali is a common language among the ethnic groups in Nepal.

Throughout Central Asia, cultures flourished and died, political boundaries changed, and religions transmogrified and evolved over the course of centuries, largely hidden from the outside world by the high peaks around them. The colonization of India gave early British explorers and surveyors what often was the first look at the amazing landscape of mountains, though some cultures and kingdoms south of the Himalaya—including Nepal—were closed completely to all outsiders until as recently as 1950.

In the midnineteenth century, Sir George Everest established the modern foundations for practical knowledge of the Himalaya when he created a carefully linked series of triangulations that provided for accurate measurements not just of the height of the great peaks of the central and eastern Himalaya, but of their positions as well. Henry Godwin-Austen joined that effort in 1857, when he explored the Karakoram, particularly the Baltoro region, where he may have become the area's first climber. Among the early expeditions to those mountains were those of Italy's Duke of Abruzzi, who, astoundingly, got within about two thousand feet (600 meters) of the summit of K2 in 1909 before being turned back by bad weather, and for whom its Abruzzi Ridge is named. British explorers Eric Shipton and Bill Tillman made a number of incredible journeys, both sepa-

▶ South Face of Lhotse
(27,923 feet/8,511 meters) ∾— Nepal

rately and together, through Central Asia from the mid-1930s to the early 1950s. Among the pair's fascinating sojourns was the first exploration of the Nanda Devi Sanctuary, which resulted in that peak's remarkable first ascent in 1936, quite early for a 25,645-foot (7,817-meter) peak. When Nepal finally opened its borders to foreigners in 1949, Shipton, in fact, made the remarkable discovery that the southern approaches to Mount Everest comprised the peak's most promising route.

The landscape itself drew these unconventional, intrepid humans to the Himalaya, and their desire to explore and climb there brought the allure of the distant region back to the Western world. But not until after World War II were the first of the world's 8,000-meter peaks actually climbed. The French were the first to succeed, when Louis Lachenal and Maurice Herzog, part of the team that included Lionel Terray and Gaston Rébuffat, reached the top of 26,504-foot (8,078-meter) Annapurna in 1950, a climb made legendary by Herzog's book of the same name. Just finding the mountain in the days before accurate maps was an achievement in itself for this pioneering expedition, and *Annapurna* became an enduring inspiration to generations of climbers and trekkers. During the ensuing decade, all of the world's highest peaks were successfully climbed: Everest, 27,923-foot (8,511-meter) Lhotse, 26,750-foot (8,153-meter) Cho Oyu, 27,824-foot (8,481-meter) Makalu, 28,169-foot (8,586-meter) Kanchenjunga, and 26,658-foot (8,125-meter) Manaslu in the Nepal Himalaya; Nanga Parbat, K2, 26,470-foot (8,068-meter) Gasherbrum II, 26,360-foot (8,035-meter) Gasherbrum I (also known as Hidden Peak), and 26,400-foot (8,047-meter) Broad Peak in the Karakoram. In Nepal 26,810-foot (8,172-meter) Dhaulagiri was climbed in 1960, and in Tibet, to which the Chinese government had closed off access in 1950, 26,286-foot (8,012-meter) Shishapangma probably first was climbed by Chinese mountaineers in 1964.

These historic ascents went far beyond mere mountain climbs; in retrospect, they can be seen as the lever that pried open the door through which significant numbers of Westerners, not just a handful of climbers, would go to the Himalaya.

The stories of those magnificent feats proved to adventurous people that they, too, could make the journey to see the Himalaya, perhaps the greatest landscape on the planet, for themselves.

There's a place on the high route between Dingboche and Lobouche, in Nepal's Khumbu region (named after the big glacier that tumbles down the southwestern flanks of Everest), where in one glance you can see three of the six highest mountains in the world: Lhotse, Makalu, and Cho Oyu. The walk is like something out of a fairy tale.

After I'd spent weeks reporting on a scientific and mountaineering expedition to the world's highest mountain, the time eventually came for me to go home. As I left the satellite phones, laptop computers, solar panels, and dispatch responsibilities with the other members of the American Everest Expedition, the change in my attitude was palpable. Suddenly no longer a journalist with deadlines, I was just a man walking through the Himalaya, on my own time, at my own pace. As I took in the view, I was reminded that having a job to do in the Himalaya is subtly different from just *being* in them, but the place works a profound magic no matter how it is experienced. Mohan, a Rai porter, and I began the 35-mile (56-kilometer) walk back to the short, steeply angled grass airstrip at Lukla, and I realized that the trek to come was a gift: all the riches of the Himalaya I could absorb in those timeless days.

Below Pheriche, we traveled south on the trail toward Thyangboche, walking through rhododendrons in magnificent full bloom and past the famous monastery there, where the head lama had blessed our group on our way into the mountain, draping a *khata* (a Buddhist religious scarf) around each person's neck. In the shadow of Thyangboche Monastery, at Mingma's teahouse, I was awakened the next morning by a chorus of strange chants, horns, and gongs. Looking out the lodge window, I saw a couple of red-robed, shaven-headed monks hanging out a second-floor window of the monastery, shouting in their strange way, blowing golden horns, and banging a small

▲   View down the Baltoro Glacier,
     Karakoram Range ᳕ Pakistan

◀   *Mani* (offering) stones, Khumbu Valley ᳕ Nepal

gong. The sky behind the monastery was a crystalline blue. I hurried outside, where the scene took my breath away. To the north, Mount Everest stood black and impossibly high above the long ridge of 25,864-foot (7,885-meter) Nuptse, while 22,486-foot (6,854-meter) Ama Dablam was a vision draped in a mantle of new snow. It's easy to see why Tillman, one of the first Europeans to come here, said, "It would be difficult to imagine a finer site for worship or contemplation."

Cruising along the trail high above the Dudh Kosi River on the way toward Namche Bazaar, we came upon a Nepalese man driving four or five laden yaks down the trail ahead of us. As is often the case, his lead animal wore a fancy red wig with tassels and baubles. The narrow trail precluded passing, so we filed along behind him as two young Sherpani (Sherpa women) came up behind us. The two girls laughed and talked together as they walked along close on our heels. The yak driver made a lot of noise, too, whistling in a continuous, oddly beautiful, steady but always shifting minor-key tone, soothing his beasts. At times he emitted sharp grunts and low yells—commands, apparently, to his laden animals. Walking between the lilting laughter of the girls behind and the mesmerizing whistles and calls of the yak wrangler ahead, I sank into a kind of hypnotized state as we passed through pine forests and rhododendron groves at about twelve thousand feet.

It was a delicious day in the Himalayan foothills, a moment in which time was completely suspended, that brought to mind my first visit to the Himalaya almost twenty years before. It's hard to say what was more affecting, the wondrous sights of Nepal and its exotic culture, or my first view of an 8,000-meter peak. Kathmandu was different then from what it is now; there were bonfires in the streets of the Thamel district at night, and pedicabs were more numerous than cars. At Bouddhanath, perhaps the biggest *stupa* (religious structure) in all the Buddhist world, I watched as the faithful walked clockwise—the direction the planets revolve around the sun—around the stupa and spun the massive bronze prayer wheels packed with ancient texts, sending out countless prayers to

the universe with every revolution. Too ignorant even to know to look for it, I stumbled by accident one full-moon night into the temple at Swayambhunath, where strange chanting drew me into a room lit by a hundred candles, the air so thick with the blue haze of incense I could hardly see the four long rows of monks—two on either side of the small room, facing each other. Their chant was mesmerizing and deeply affecting.

My first venture outside the capital into the backcountry of the Himalaya introduced me to the profound pleasure of walking day after day through a pastoral countryside unlike any other on Earth. From the higher ridges came those first, unforgettable close-up views of peaks among the magnificent Annapurna Range. The view on the way out, toward the city of Pokhara, was dominated by 22,956-foot (6,997-meter) Machapuchare, which rivals Ama Dablam as the most beautiful of mountains. Those views fueled whatever is in me that loves mountains.

Now, two decades later, Mohan and I were almost to Lukla when, at a place called Ghat, we came upon soaring prayer-flag poles beside a couple of huge boulders brightly painted with the classic Buddhist mantra *om mani padme hum* (which translates "hail to the jewel in the lotus"). I paused there, at the end of that journey, feeling fortunate to have come this time in the company of climbers, old hands whose insight into the people and landscape of the Himalaya changed the way I saw everything.

The best climbers are a lot like the rest of us except that they are more susceptible to the power of big mountains and work harder at getting proficient about being in them. So when they go to the Himalaya, they go farther, higher, and more frequently, often coming back with a master's perspective—not just because of where they've been, but *how* they've been there: with commitment, often with their lives in the balance. That hard-won outlook inspired me to ask some of the great climbers what they think—not about climbing, but about the Himalaya, and a lifetime spent among the mountains and the people there.

▶ Worshippers at Bouddhanath Stupa,
Kathmandu ∾ Nepal

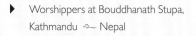

▲ Shepherd ∾ Tibet

REINHOLD MESSNER

In 1970, an unknown twenty-five-year-old climber from the South Tyrol of Italy went on his first journey to the Himalaya. Already an accomplished Alpine climber, with an impressive list of solo ascents and the big north walls of the Alps behind him, Reinhold Messner felt ready for the Rupal face of Nanga Parbat. From Rawalpindi, Pakistan, the expedition flew on to Gilgit, 400 miles (650 kilometers) north, and continued by jeep and foot finally into the Rupal Valley of northern Pakistan, with more than 300 porters to carry equipment. The huge face loomed above, three times the size of the Alps' Eiger Nordwand, a route so intimidating that Hermann Buhl, who first climbed Nanga Parbat, had called the face "unclimbable."

After weeks of slow progress in bad weather establishing the route, Messner and his brother Gunther finally were poised for the summit push from high camp. The pair climbed quickly, and by late afternoon reached the top of the face and the summit. But the brothers, unable to descend the difficult technical ground they had come up, were caught out high on the mountain overnight and forced to bivouac. Eventually they had to descend via the Diamir face, on a completely different side of Nanga Parbat, where the climbers became separated. Gunther was not seen again, and Reinhold himself barely survived. The epic descent necessitated yet another exposed bivouac, freezing his toes.

An exhausted and delirious Messner finally crawled down into the upper reaches of the Diamir Valley on the opposite side of the mountain from where he had set out. Hobbling

Reinhold Messner Collection

on his ruined feet, he met woodcutters who fed him and led him to the village of Diamirai. Armed men approached, but instead of robbing Messner, they carried him to safety. Reunited with the other members of his expedition, Messner returned to Europe, where his frozen toes were amputated.

Despite the tragic circumstances, Messner's climb on Nanga Parbat was historic, a new route and a traverse of the 8,000-meter peak. Although grief over the death of his brother never really left him, the experience was a formative one for Messner—not just his first meaningful encounter with the people of a distant mountain culture, but the beginnings of a life spent largely among the high peaks of the Himalaya. In the decades that followed, Messner returned to the big mountains of Central Asia more frequently than almost any other Western climber, making ascents in every corner of the range, sometimes just trekking through remote regions, always making friends in many cultures. It was the only place, says Messner, that he felt at home.

Messner's stunning achievements throughout the Himalaya would so torque the world of big-peak mountaineering as to make it unrecognizable. In 1975 Messner began changing the style in which mountains were climbed when he made the first alpine-style ascent of an 8,000-meter mountain, Hidden Peak, in the Karakoram of Pakistan. In alpine-style, the climb is done without established camps but in a single push, with everything the climber needs in his pack. Three years later, he climbed the south side of Everest from

◀ Thamserkhu, Khumbu Valley ∿ Nepal

◀◀ Himalayan vista from Kala Pattar (18,187 feet/ 5,545 meters), Khumbu Valley ∿ Nepal

Nepal without oxygen, the first time that had been done. His goal was to prove that human beings could climb an 8,000-meter peak without supplemental oxygen—as he put it, "by fair means." Two years after, he made a solo ascent of Everest (from base camp to summit), another first, from its north side via Tibet. In the space of five years, the "taboos of mountaineering," as he calls them, had fallen before him. Perhaps the final monumental landmark Messner would set came in 1986, when his ascent of Lhotse in Nepal made him the first person to have climbed all fourteen of the world's 8,000-meter peaks.

Messner is not unmindful of the scale of his achievements, but it is the people he encountered along the way who made the greatest impression. "The contact I had with the peoples of Nepal, Pakistan, and India," Messner told me from Dessau, Germany, in February 2001, "had a particularly strong impact on me. I felt a kinship with these people from the very beginning. I was always seeking to live with them, to know how they handled their lives, to learn how they survived the harsh circumstances. I was interested because I too grew up in a mountain world, living in the rural Alps. I believe that I had a common ground that perhaps other climbers or travelers never had. I understood these new cultures quite quickly, more quickly than other Western climbers did.

"This is what is common among all the mountain people over the world. They have different languages, different religions, different philosophies, and of course different laws because they live in different countries, but their feeling, their attitude toward the mountains, is the same: I think that when you go to the mountains and live with these people, you are not a Buddhist or Christian or Muslim, but a human being, and the focus is the same for everyone.

"The friendships I have with Himalayan people have enriched my life," he said, "but it is important to know that when I speak about my experiences with the local people, what I feel most strongly about is *their* life in *their* home, and not my reaction to it. When we are in base camps in the high country, we all live the same way, drink from the same cup, eat the same food, which does not tell me who my Pakistani friends or my Sherpa friends really are. After many of my expeditions, I accompanied my friends to their homes and spent a week or two with them to see how they really lived, to see their wives and their kids, their small cattle and their houses—all over the Himalaya. This has given me a strong relationship with these people."

Recognition for Messner's climbing accomplishments, especially among people who know and love the mountain world, make him powerful in other ways. An elected member of the European Parliament since 1999, and the successful author of more than a dozen books, Messner is increasingly using both his political office and his tremendous personal influence on behalf of the peoples of the Himalaya with whom he has become so close.

"Hunzas, Baltis, Sherpas, Tibetans, all the people I have met in the Himalaya," he says, "have two things in common: their feelings toward the landscape, and their sense of self-sufficiency. That gives them a kind of freedom, but not the freedom that allows for unfettered movement. If you have a yak herd, you have to tend the herd every day; it's like being in jail. But these people have a freedom in their mind because they are completely self-sufficient, able to survive, to handle the realities of their life every day. This kind of freedom, this self-sufficiency, demands a lot of knowledge, which we have lost in our Western communities."

Messner is convinced there is a way to help the economically poorer mountain cultures of the Himalaya benefit from the rich experiences they offer the rest of us. He sees the beginnings of a kind of exchange that might enrich both worlds, a way for people of wealthier countries to reap the rewards of experiences in these mountain areas while at the same time benefiting the people who live there.

"I would like to give to the Westerners—the Americans, the Japanese, the Europeans, the people from the rich countries—a more balanced approach to these areas," Messner says. "They should go there not only to climb or enjoy the

▲ Grandfather and child, Askole village, Baltoro region ⌒ Pakistan

▶ Shepherd, Kashgar ⌒ China

Himalaya; they should go there also to understand the culture and the people who live there. It's beautiful to see Everest—and, for me, even better to climb it—and those experiences can be priceless. But it's at least as important when we stay among these communities that we make the effort to understand them. At the same time that we get something from them, we can help them. I think this approach is essential if we are to preserve those cultures and the experience we go there for.

"I know these issues from direct experience," he says, "and not just in the Himalaya, but here at home too. What's happening in the Himalaya is not that different from what is happening here in the Alps. For the past fifty years we have been living more or less on tourism, but even here we have seen in the past few decades that there are only a few areas where tourism can be successful enough to provide a living—and, tragically, in those few areas tourism is destroying the very landscape that has generated it. I would like to try to help in a political way, to arrive at a solution that brings a greater balance between both the local culture and the tourism industry that relies on it."

As Messner speaks off the cuff about difficult issues in the Himalaya, his thoughtful and open earnestness make him seem far different from his persona as the arrogant European *wunderkind* who seemingly brought the highest mountains on Earth down to a human scale. Now Messner is in even greater demand around the world as a lecturer and speaker than he was during his heyday in the 1970s and '80s, when his climbing feats transformed mountaineering standards. But the people and places of the Himalaya are so close to the climber's heart that he is willing to give of his besieged time and attention if he thinks it might help. Which is why Messner talked to me from the Astrom Hotel even as his "hosts" were trying to drag him off to be on time for the evening lecture.

"It's a signal that I'm getting older, for sure, that I am now turning my attention to helping the Himalayan people," Messner says. "But this is very important. It is my hope—and

now my work—that the climbers and trekkers who go to the Himalaya understand that we not only have the opportunity for great, life-changing experiences from these hills and the people who live in them, but we also can go there and give something back."

Reinhold Messner has turned his fearlessness, strength, and sense of commitment to protecting the mountains of Central Asia. He points to the Sherpa people of Nepal as an example of what can be done, a kind of guide map to giving something back to the cultures of the place where he made his mountaineering achievements.

"Sherpas are better off today, much more so than in 1953 when Sir Edmund Hillary went to Everest," Messner says. "Many Sherpa are now prosperous from the lucrative tourism industry—not so rich as Europeans or Americans, perhaps, and so you could say that, in some respects, we are living a better life. In other respects, however, such as those of strong family bonds and personal contentment, their life could be judged to be better, more whole, more complete.

"But the Sherpas are the exception in the Himalaya. They are lucky to have Everest, which many tourists, trekkers, and climbers want to visit, and in some ways that reflects the unique qualities of openness and friendliness that shape their culture. Many Westerners who go to Everest end up being affected by the Sherpa culture, and so try to give something back by helping the Sherpa people."

However, the relative affluence of *some* Sherpas should not be taken as a gauge of the state of other Himalayan peoples.

"That's an exception," Messner emphasizes. "In general most mountain people around the world have seen little improvement in their economic condition, and some are even getting poorer. That's a big problem. Tourism, trekking, and climbing could be of great benefit for all mountain people around the world, if we can do it in the right way, in a balanced way.

"Tourists should be dispersed among the mountain areas

▲ Woman, Kathmandu ∾ Nepal   ◀ Detail of a hand, Kathmandu ∾ Nepal to minimize impact and yet still bring significant currency to the local people, just as has happened with the Sherpas in Nepal. If the local people spend this money in the right way, they could slowly improve their life in significant ways."

The example Messner cites of the Sherpas also demonstrates that people who benefit from an experience in the Himalaya often are willing to give something back. Climbers who return to the Himalaya year after year cannot help but be more deeply affected, according to Messner, than more casual visitors.

"I think that, as climbers, we have seen these people in a way that few others have," he says. "We have gone, season after season, into the mountains and have seen year in and year out how these people live, and so we know who they are. With that greater exposure, it's only natural that we are moved to respond.

"It's very important that we care about these places and these people. It is much more important to care about the mountain people of the Himalaya than it is to care about the snow on the summit of Everest.

"Native people of the mountain areas should still handle their lands in traditional ways, and be self-sufficient with crops

and beasts of burden such as yaks, but then also have the revenue from assisting trekkers and climbers. That could be a second economic leg on which to stand. In the end, we would have a greater balance between both the local culture and tourism that might benefit everyone. It is my hope to encourage this."

Messner has not forgotten the kindness shown to him more than thirty years ago in a faraway place called the Diamir Valley, or the people he described as handsome and friendly despite the pervasive poverty and sickness in the remote valley.

"I am in the process of building a school in the valley below Nanga Parbat," he says, with obvious relish. "It was the scene of my most desperate circumstance, where I barely survived in 1970 after my Nanga Parbat traverse. These are still very poor people. The school I am building there will be ready in 2002.

"I will never lose contact with the people of that valley, and the other people of the Himalaya who have become my friends," he says. "To give something to them, to help them in some way, gives a good feeling to us. It is beneficial for those of us who have been there to share what we have in abundance with those who have shared so much with us."

▲ Gasherbrum I (26,470 feet/8,068 meters), Karakoram Range ᠕— Pakistan

▶ Mount Everest and a crescent moon ᠕— Tibet

Rongbuk Glacier ᔢ Tibet

Androsace tapete, Rongbuk Valley ᴐ— Tibet

House detail, Tash Kurghan ᷍ Western China   ▲   Uighur woman on the road, Kashgar ᷍ China

Granite cliffs above the Baltoro Glacier, Trango Tower Region, and the Karakoram Range ◦⁓ Pakistan

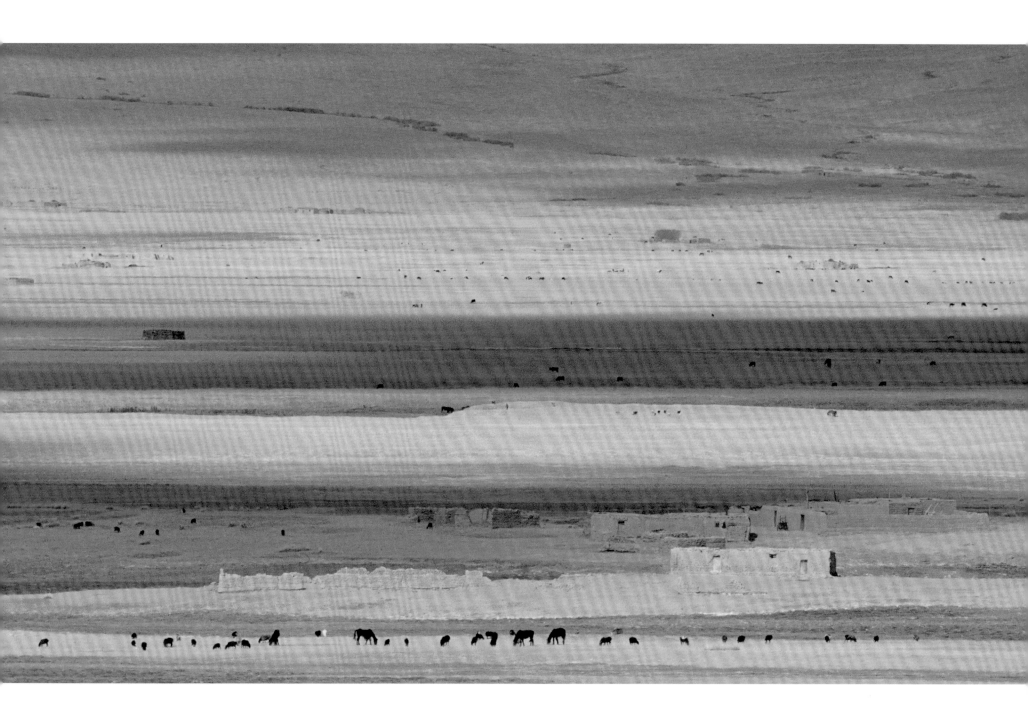

Pamir Plateau, Himalayan Range ๛ China

◀ Footbridge above the Hunza River ∽ Pakistan   ▲ Uighur man on a donkey cart, Kashgar ∽ China   31

◀ ▲ Lower slopes of Nuptse (22,494 feet/7,861 meters),
Khumbu Valley 〜 Nepal

34   ▲ Seracs, Rongbuk Glacier ᔭ— Tibet   ▶ Banded rock, Baltoro Glacier ᔭ— Pakistan

▲   Mount Everest and Nuptse ⁓ Nepal   ▶   Moonset over Lingtren ⁓ Tibetan-Nepalese border

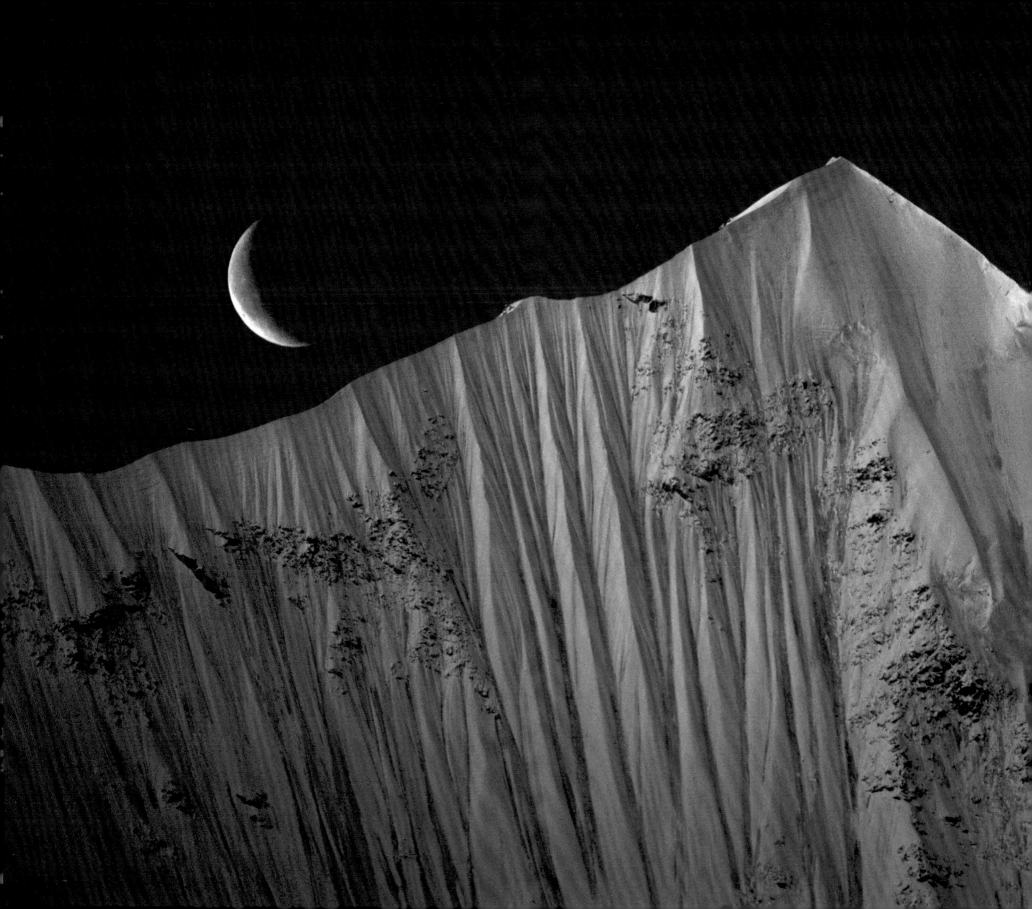

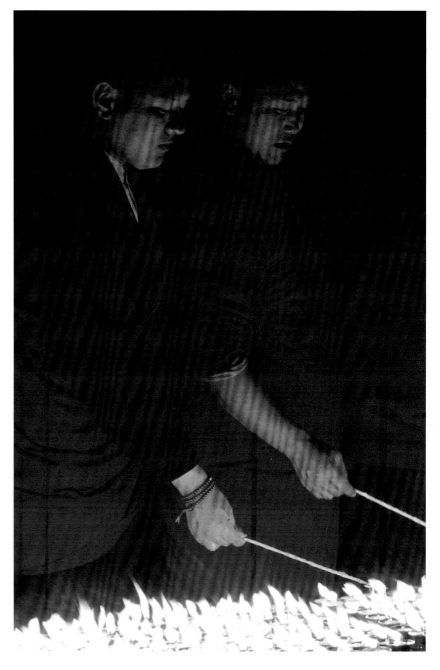

38   ▲   Everest Base Camp, Rongbuk Valley ☙ Tibet

▲ ▶   Buddhist monks and candles, Bouddhanath Stupa,
Kathmandu ☙ Nepal

Bouddhanath Stupa, Kathmandu ⌒ Nepal

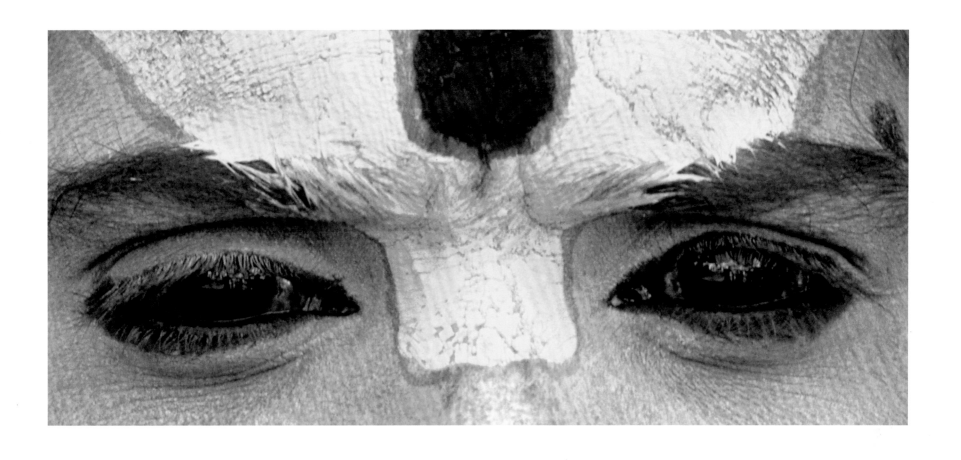

Naga sadhu (Hindu holy man), Hindu temple,
Kathmandu ⌒ Nepal

Wall mural, Potala Palace, Lhasa ⁓ Tibet

▲ Rama and ▶ Sita, Hindu temple, Kathmandu ∽– Nepal

44 ▲ Uighur children, Kashgar ∽ China   ▶ Mountain children, Karimabad, Hunza Valley ∽ Pakistan

▲ ▶ Uighur children, Xekar ⌖ China

K2 (28,250 feet/8,611 meters) from Concordia,
Karakoram Range ∼ Pakistan

Mount Everest ∽ Tibet

50   ▲   *Waldheimia stoliczkai*, Baltoro Glacier ☙— Pakistan

▲   Buddhist stupa below Thamserkhu ☙— Nepal
▶   The town of Namche Bazaar ☙— Nepal

▲ Nepalese home interior, Namche Bazaar ⌇ Nepal   ▶ Guesthouse, Pheriche, Khumbu region ⌇ Nepal

▲ House detail, Pokhara region ᵔ Nepal
◀ Tibetan girl, Xigazê ᵔ Tibet

▲ House detail, Taklimakan Desert ᵔ China

▲ A young harvester, Askole village ✌ Pakistan   ▶ Terraced mustard fields, Himalayan foothills ✌ Nepal

Mitre Peak (19,767 feet/6,025 meters),
Karakoram Range ✑ Pakistan

PHOTOGRAPHER'S FIELD NOTES

Pages 18–19

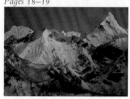

Ama Dablam, Nepal
One of my most memorable moments in the high Himalaya came as I stood atop Kala Pattar, a rock promontory rising above Nepal's Khumbu Valley base camps of Everest. From Kala Pattar's summit there are spectacular views in all directions. Here Ama Dablam dominates the vista.

Nikon F3, Nikkor 200–400mm lens, f/4 at 1/30 second, polarizing filter, Fujichrome 100 film

Page 24

Rongbuk Glacier, Tibet
Higher up on Everest, the surface of the Rongbuk Glacier is smooth with freshly fallen snow. But as the glacier creeps down the valley toward Tibet, its surface becomes spectacularly fractured, and traversing it is all but impossible.

Nikon F3, Nikkor 200–400mm lens, f/16 at 1/60 second, Kodachrome 64 film

Page 25

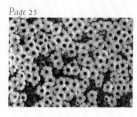

Androsace tapete, Tibet
I passed from winter into spring during my three-month stay in the Rongbuk Valley on Everest's north side. I began to suspect that no flowers existed in this harsh, arid environment until I stumbled across these tiny *Androsace tapete* blossoms growing so close to the rocks that it would have been easy to overlook them.

Nikon F3, Nikkor 55mm macro lens, f/16 at 1/2 second, Kodachrome 64 film

Page 26

Tash Kurghan, Western China
Homes in the Himalaya come in all forms, from rock caves to brick and adobe to wood. Here the walls consist of the trunks of poplar trees. Stacks of yak dung—a primary source of fuel—dry at the base of the wall.

Nikon F3, Nikkor 80–200mm lens, f/11 at 1/60 second, Fujichrome 50 film

Page 27

Kashgar, China
At the base of the Himalaya, rows of Himalayan poplar trees (*Populus ciliata*) are often planted along rural roads. These dense rows provide villages with protection from the high winds that frequently blow down the slopes. Here a Muslim Uighur woman stands in front of a row of poplars.

Nikon F3, Nikkor 200–400mm lens, f/22 at 1/2 second, Fujichrome 100 film

Page 28

Trango Tower region, Pakistan
Late-afternoon light illuminates dust particles blown into the air by the strong winds that swirl around Trango Tower in the Karakoram Range.

Canon EOS-1N, Canon EF 400mm lens, f/8 at 1/60 second, Fujichrome Velvia film

Page 29

Pamir Plateau, China
In stark contrast to the vertical world of the high Himalaya, the Pamir Plateau a short distance beyond is a mountainous "knot" in Central Asia from which the five great mountain ranges of Asia radiate: the Himalaya, Karakoram, Hindu Kush, Tien Shan, and Kunlun Shan. The plateau provides ample forage for small herds of goats, sheep, camels, and yaks.

Nikon F3, Nikkor 400mm lens, f/11 at 1/60 second, Fujichrome 50 film

Page 30

Hunza River, Pakistan
A footbridge a bit past its prime spans the swift waters of the Hunza River. I was always amazed to see villagers confidently crossing bridges that looked like they were put together with chewing gum.

Nikon F3, Nikkor 80–200mm lens, f/11 at 1/60 second, Fujichrome 100 film

Page 31

Kashgar, China
A Uighur man, one of China's many minorities, guides his donkey down a rural road in Kashgar on the western border of China.

Nikon F3, Nikkor 80–200mm lens, f/8 at 1/125 second, Fujichrome 50 film

Pages 32, 33

Nuptse, Nepal
Glaciated ridges rise steeply above the Khumbu Glacier on the lower slopes of Nuptse. As the light deepens in the late afternoon, the textures of the many avalanche paths are emphasized on this steep ridge of ice- and snow-covered rock.

Page 32: Nikon F3, Nikkor 80–200mm lens, f/11 at 1/30 second, Fujichrome 50 film
Page 33: Nikon F3, Nikkor 80–200mm lens, f/8 at 1/2 second, Fujichrome 50 film

Page 34

Rongbuk Glacier, Tibet
Seracs are a striking feature of some glaciers. They stand 30 to 40 feet (9 to 12 meters) tall, a formidable obstacle for trekkers. I used a zoom lens to fill the frame and remove any sense of scale, making these seracs on the Rongbuk Glacier look as dramatic as a range of mountain peaks.

Nikon F3, Nikkor 200–400mm lens, f/16 at 1/30 second, Kodachrome 64 film

Page 35

Baltoro Glacier, Pakistan
Beautiful bands of minerals caught my eye as I passed a small boulder lying atop the Baltoro Glacier. Dislodged from the slopes above, this boulder will ultimately be transported many miles down the valley by the slow-moving glacier.

Canon EOS-1N, Canon EF 100mm lens, f/16 at 1/30 second, Fujichrome Velvia film

Page 36

Everest and Nuptse, Nepal
The afterglow of a sunset bathes the summits of Everest and Nuptse in soft hues as the temperature drops steeply with the fading light. I photographed this image from the summit of Nepal's Kala Pattar.

Nikon F3, Nikkor 80–200mm lens, f/8 at 1/2 second, Fujichrome 50 film

Page 37

Lingtren, Tibetan-Nepalese border
One of my favorite subjects to photograph during my three months on Everest was the pyramidal Lingtren peak perched on the Tibetan-Nepalese border. In this photo, the crescent moon sets in the predawn light of a May morning.

Nikon F3, Nikkor 400mm lens, f/4 at 1/8 second, Kodachrome 64 film

Page 38, left

Mount Everest, Tibet
The climbers' tents in the Rongbuk Valley base camp are illuminated by lantern light, while Mount Everest, partially illuminated by moonlight, looms above.

Nikon F3, Nikkor 80–200 lens, f/2.8 at 10 minutes, Kodachrome 64 film

Page 38, right, and 39

Kathmandu, Nepal
Monks from the Tashi Samtenling Monastery light candles in veneration of the Buddha at the Bouddhanath Stupa. Light symbolizes wisdom and darkness, ignorance. To determine the proper exposure, I spot-read the light level reflecting off the monks' faces; for the candles, I spot-read off the rim of one candleholder.

Page 38: Canon EOS-3, Canon EF 70–200mm lens, f/4 at 1/8 second, Fujichrome Provia film
Page 39: Canon EOS-3, Canon EF 70–200mm lens, f/22 at 2 seconds, Fujichrome Provia film

Page 40

Kathmandu, Nepal
The Bouddhanath Stupa has become the center of culture and education for both the Tibetan and the Nepalese Buddhists residing in Kathmandu.

Canon EOS-3, Canon EF 70–200mm lens, f/16 at 1/15 second, polarizing filter, Fujichrome Velvia film

Page 41

Kathmandu, Nepal
Sadhus are Hindu holy men, and the Naga order is the most rigorous. A Naga sadhu has no desire for clothing, sex, or money. He must be ready to die any time for the cause of Hinduism. The ash on this Naga sadhu's body symbolizes his readiness to perish. He is the "warrior-ascetic" of Hinduism.

Canon EOS-1N, Canon EF 70–200mm lens, f/11 at 1/30 second, Fujichrome Velvia film

Page 42

Lhasa, Tibet
The hundreds of murals gracing the halls and corridors of the Potala Palace were painted in the seventeenth century. Most of them depict the history of Tibetan Buddhism. Others describe the construction of the Potala as well as the folk customs of various historical periods. The Potala, the former palace of the Dalai Lama, has always been a pilgrimage destination.

Nikon F3, Nikkor 80–200mm lens, f/16 at 1/60 second, flash, Kodachrome 64 film

Page 43, left and right

Kathmandu, Nepal
The epic poem "The Ramayana" is the oldest, most popular mythological story in India. It tells how Rama (left), the incarnation of Lord Vishnu, rids the Earth of Ravana, the ten-headed demon king of Lanka. Sita (right), Rama's beautiful wife, is kidnapped by Ravana, and a fierce battle ensues, in which good triumphs over evil.

Both: Canon EOS-3, Canon EF 70–200mm lens, f/11 at 1/15 second, fill flash, Fujichrome Velvia film

Page 44

Kashgar, China
Although part of China, Kashgar is dominated by the Muslim Uighur people. Kashgar was established along the Silk Road, which linked Asia and Europe. The heritage of both continents can be seen in the faces of these children.

Canon F-1, Canon FD 80–200mm lens, f/11 at 1/125 second, Fujichrome 100 film

Page 45

Karimabad, Pakistan
The children of Karimabad are like children anywhere, curious, eager to investigate anything new that comes their way—in this instance, me. I find that first photographing the children of a new place often paves the way for interacting with the adults later.

Canon F-1, Canon FD 20mm lens, f/11 at 1/30 second, 2-stop graduated neutral density filter, Fujichrome 100 film

Pages 46, 47

Xekar, China
As I wandered through the narrow streets of Xekar, a small town on the northwestern side of the Taklimakan Desert, Uighur children cautiously peered through an open passageway. Because the direct sun was too harsh for my taste, I used the reflected light bouncing off the sunlit walls.

Both: Canon F-1, Canon FD 80–200mm lens, f/4 at 1/30 second, Fujichrome 100 film

Page 48

K2, Pakistan
K2, the world's second-highest mountain, as seen from Concordia, is framed by the valley of the Godwin-Austen Glacier in the Karakoram. Late-afternoon light highlights K2's western face.

Canon EOS-1N, Canon EF 80–200mm lens, f/22 at 1/15 second, polarizing filter, Fujichrome Velvia film

Page 49

Mount Everest, Tibet
Within Tibet, Everest is known as Chomolungma, which means "Mother Goddess of the Land." In this photo, taken from base camp in Tibet, Chomolungma's famous Yellow Band, a 700-foot horizontal bed of striated golden limestone beneath the Northeast Ridge, is clearly visible.

Nikon F3, Nikkor 400mm lens, Nikon 1.4x teleconverter, f/8 at 1/125 second, Kodachrome 64 film

Page 50, left

Wildflowers, Pakistan
A large clump of hardy *Waldheimia stoliczkai* flourishes in the warm temperatures atop the Baltoro Glacier. In many places, so much rock and earth cover the surface of the glacier that vegetation can grow.

Canon EOS-1N, Canon EF 100mm Macro lens, f/16 at 1/30 second, Fujichrome Velvia film

Page 50, right

Thamserkhu, Nepal
A stupa is a commemorative monument usually housing sacred relics associated with the Buddha or other saintly persons. It is an architectural symbol of the Buddha's *parinirvana*, or death. A stupa is silhouetted against the mists rising from the valleys below. Above and in the distance, the summit of Thamserkhu catches the last rays of the descending sun.

Nikon F3, Nikkor 80–200mm lens, f/16 at 1/8 second, polarizing filter, Fujichrome 100 film

Page 51

Namche Bazaar, Nepal
The thriving town of Namche Bazaar provides an important resting place for trekkers and climbing expeditions en route to Everest's south side. As expeditions exit the mountains after completing their climbs, leftover equipment, food, and clothing end up in the local shops of Namche Bazaar.

Nikon F3, Nikkor 20mm lens, f/22 at 1/8 second, Fujichrome 100 film

Page 52

Namche Bazaar, Nepal
Large metal pans reflect the light from a tiny window in a private home in Namche Bazaar. The home is owned by the parents of a man we met in Kathmandu. He invited us to stay the night. A small photograph on a wall showed that Jimmy and Roslyn Carter had also stayed in this same home.

Nikon F3, Nikkor 20mm lens, f/16 at 2 seconds, Kodachrome 64 film

Page 53

Pheriche, Nepal
A trekker sips a cup of yak's-milk tea within the smoky interior of a guesthouse in Pheriche, in the Khumbu region. The interiors of most homes are filled with the smoke of fires fueled either by juniper wood or yak dung. Many villagers suffer from chronic lung congestion as a result.

Nikon F3, Nikkor 20mm lens, f/16 at 1 second, Fujichrome 100 film

Page 54

Xigazê, Tibet
A Tibetan teenager peers inquisitively into the jeep transporting us to the Everest base camp in the Rongbuk Valley. In 1984, relatively few Westerners had been permitted to travel through this region of Tibet. Local Tibetans were fascinated not only by our Western faces, but also by everything that we carried—from clothes to cameras to audio cassettes.

Nikon F3, Nikkor 80–200mm lens, f/4 at 1/60 second, Kodachrome 64 film

Page 55, left

Pokhara region, Nepal
October is the time for preparing recently harvested crops in the small mountain villages above Pokhara. Corn is typically dried from the rafters of the well-constructed houses.

Nikon F3, Nikkor 80–200mm lens, f/11 at 1/15 second, Fujichrome 100 film

Page 55, right

Taklimakan Desert, China
Mud and clay are the building materials of the desert. Wood is scarce, as is glass. Houses are built to withstand the high winds and blowing sands of the desert.

Canon F-1, Canon FD 80–200mm lens, f/16 at 1/30 second, Fujichrome 50 film

Page 56

Askole village, Pakistan
A youth carries a large basket of wildflowers that were grown along the Biaho Lungpa River. The forage will be dried, stored, then fed to livestock during the long winter months.

Canon F-1, Canon FD 80–200mm lens, f/11 at 1/60 second, Fujichrome Velvia film

Page 57

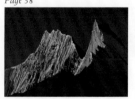

Himalayan foothills, Nepal
Harvesters take to the fields to collect mustard in the fertile Himalayan valleys of Nepal. To gain a more interesting perspective, I climbed an adjacent hillside, where the elevated view enabled me to convey the textures and lines of the fields.

Canon EOS-3, Canon EF 70–200mm lens, f/16 at 1/30 second, polarizing filter, Fujichrome Velvia film

Page 58

Mitre Peak, Pakistan
In the Karakoram, Mitre Peak's western face glows in the late-afternoon light. Its razor-sharp summit ridge is clearly delineated by the low angle of the sun's rays.

Canon EOS-1N, Canon EF 400mm lens, f/16 at 1/30 second, Fujichrome Velvia film

ED VIESTURS

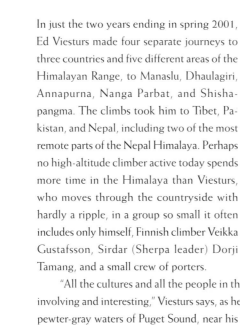

Ed Viesturs Collection

In just the two years ending in spring 2001, Ed Viesturs made four separate journeys to three countries and five different areas of the Himalayan Range, to Manaslu, Dhaulagiri, Annapurna, Nanga Parbat, and Shisha-pangma. The climbs took him to Tibet, Pakistan, and Nepal, including two of the most remote parts of the Nepal Himalaya. Perhaps no high-altitude climber active today spends more time in the Himalaya than Viesturs, who moves through the countryside with hardly a ripple, in a group so small it often includes only himself, Finnish climber Veikka Gustafsson, Sirdar (Sherpa leader) Dorji Tamang, and a small crew of porters.

"All the cultures and all the people in these countries are involving and interesting," Viesturs says, as he gazes across the pewter-gray waters of Puget Sound, near his home in Seattle, Washington. "Sometimes I really can't believe how fortunate I am that what I do has taken me to these places."

Viesturs, who has reached the summit of Everest five times, became well known during the 1990s as he neared the end of his attempt to climb all fourteen of the world's 8,000-meter peaks without oxygen. His fame was cemented, however, by disastrous events high on Everest in 1996, when eight climbers died in a single storm.

That year Viesturs was the climbing leader for a large IMAX film crew, responsible for the food, equipment, and logistics of getting them all to Everest, where he was to be among the "talent" in a large-format film being shot by American climber and filmmaker David Breashears. While Viesturs and the rest of the team were at Camp II, above the Khumbu Icefall in the Western Cwm, a sudden deadly storm struck other parties high on the mountain, taking the lives of guided-expedition leaders Scott Fischer from the United States, Rob Hall from New Zealand, and three of Hall's clients and guides. Viesturs, Breashears, and other IMAX team members moved up the mountain to assist the stricken survivors, and with American climbers Pete Athans and Todd Burleson, they helped guide two injured climbers down to the Western Cwm. From there, they were evacuated by Nepalese military pilot Madan K.C. in one of the highest-altitude helicopter retrievals in the Himalaya, from 20,000 feet (6,000 meters).

In the wake of the tragedy, Viesturs said it was important that his team not give up, that the film be completed. "I felt that if we went home after the storm, we would leave this pall of death over the mountain," Viesturs says, "leaving people to think of Everest as this killer mountain. But mountains aren't like that; they just *are*, and it's your own actions that result in either a good or deadly experience. I wanted to show people we could safely climb the mountain and safely come back down."

I first met the personable and articulate Viesturs in 1991 while I was reporting on Himalayan climbing, but got to know him much better in 1998 when I asked him to provide firsthand reports of his climbs via satellite telephone to *MountainZone.com* as worldwide interest in Himalayan climbing exploded. Because on his private climbs Viesturs won't tolerate the presence of big groups, film crews, or a lot of computer hardware—all of which he feels detract from the intimate relationship he has with the big mountains of the Himalaya—another solution had to be found. I eventually sent him off to the Himalaya with the smallest satellite phone then in existence and plenty of batteries. His twice-daily telephone calls, often from near the summit of some of the wildest and highest peaks on Earth, were among the most dramatic ever broadcast.

Viesturs, with his partner, Gustafsson, has developed a style of climbing that accentuates athleticism and minimizes the time spent up high—thereby reducing the element of danger. The two climbers maintain such a fine edge of fitness and climbing skill that, once acclimated, they can attempt two 8,000-meter peaks back to back. Such was the case in 1999, when Viesturs went to the Nepal Himalaya to climb seldom-visited Manaslu, followed immediately by Dhaulagiri, 75 miles (120 kilometers) to the southeast.

"I think Nepal offers everything we go to the Himalaya for—the mountains, an exotic culture so different from home, and lots of time in the countryside," Viesturs says. "And Manaslu was probably the wildest place. That area is pristine and remote; in fact, it's so close to the Tibetan border you need special permits to go there. For me, it's one of the most exotic places in that part of the Himalaya.

"Veikka and I were constantly amazed at both the openness of the culture and how quickly a rapport and trust is established between total strangers," Viesturs continues. "Dorji, a Tamang who goes with Veikka and me on most trips lately as our Sirdar and cook—he knows us and we know him—was with us. We trekked along through the countryside without seeing another Westerner for days. When we pulled into a village, Dorji found some farmer's house, knocked on the door, and asked if he could use their outdoor kitchen. I've never seen anyone turn him down.

"The way it works is, Dorji uses their fire to cook dinner. We might spend some time in the house with the whole fam-

ily. The kids look at us like we're from Mars, these strange, pale dudes. But they are friendly and seem genuinely inviting, and we look back at them with just as much curiosity, equally amazed. Rural Nepal is strikingly warm and friendly. After dinner, we usually sleep in the barn or in a nearby shed, or pitch a tent outside."

Viesturs says his trek to Manaslu was "just a fabulous way to experience the mountains. It's so easy, too, because we eat regular Sherpa food, rice and dahl (lentils), that sort of thing, so Dorji just makes what he'd make for himself anyway. We don't hassle with pasta or other Western foods that a lot of trekkers and climbers seem to want. It's all very easy, familiar, and relaxing; it fits well with the culture.

"The last inhabited place before base camp was a place called Somagon, where Tibetan people come across the border into Nepal. When you arrive at Somagon, you have to let all your lowland porters go and hire these temporary residents, so we had women and kids jostling for a chance to take a day off from the potato fields and carry a load up to Manaslu base camp. These people have the traits of pure ethnic Tibetans, the clothing and silver jewelry. When we arrived at base camp, they dropped their loads and began laughing, singing, and dancing. It was like a day off to them, think of it, and they had each carried 60 pounds (28 kilograms) up to base camp.

"I'm not so focused on the climbing that I can't appreciate the landscape and the people on the way in. Obviously, my goal is to get to the mountain, but if it's going to take a week or two of walking to get there, that's just part of the larger experience."

Viesturs and Gustafsson took eighteen days after reaching base camp to acclimate and climb Manaslu. Acclimatization is achieved by making repeated trips up high to establish camps, and returning to base camp for rest. While listening to Viesturs, I had to pay close attention to catch the climbing details. The actual mountaineering is such an intrinsic part of his personality that he understates it, making it seem easy, a foregone conclusion, when in fact the physical challenge is

▲ Trekkers, Khumbu Valley ~ Nepal   ▶ Transporting crops, Kashgar ~ China

somewhere beyond the imagination, even for most climbers. After climbing 26,658-foot (8,125-meter) Manaslu, the pair flew by helicopter to Dhaulagiri, preserving their hard-won acclimatization, and immediately took on the 26,810-foot (8,172-meter) mountain as if they were off for a weekend trip in Washington State's Cascades. In a single push, the two men climbed the sixth-highest mountain in the world alpine-style in three days.

"That's what it is about for me," Viesturs says with a wide grin and almost boyish relish, "hookin' up and goin' and doin' it."

Viesturs, who had a long apprenticeship as a guide on Washington State's Mount Rainier while studying to be a veterinarian, knows how to gauge the risk of objective dangers—avalanche, falling rocks, the sorts of realities from which all the skill in the world can't protect you. Only judgment can do that, and his combination of skill and judgment are what Viesturs considers his most valuable assets on a big mountain. "The one time when I think I probably crossed the line, and crossed it big time," he says, "was on K2."

A thousand feet or so (a few hundred meters) lower than Mount Everest, the Karakoram giant is universally considered by experienced climbers to be far more difficult and dangerous. Viesturs went to K2 in 1992 in the company of fellow American guide Scott Fischer, and the pair's experience there devolved into an endless series of desperate challenges. First, Fischer fell into a crevasse early in the climb, his fall stopped only by Viestur's belay—when he quickly anchored the rope to which both men were tied. Weeks later, the pair was caught in an avalanche during a rescue attempt below the peak's notorious Camp IV, the scene of multiple tragic deaths over the past decades. Nearing the top, Viesturs and Fischer had to abandon their own summit attempt to aid a climber who had become exhausted and snowblind.

After that, incredibly, Fischer and Viesturs climbed back up to their previous high point and on to the high camp on the Abruzzi Ridge. There they were joined by Colorado climber Charlie Mace, and the three pushed on through marginal weather to reach the dangerous and elusive summit, nearly two months after Viesturs and Fischer had arrived at the mountain. Once on top, the climbers watched, aghast, as clouds rolled in and snow began to fall. Descending from Camp IV on K2 is often impossible in bad weather; from the summit, their chances were even more remote. Snow covered the footprints they had made on the way up, leaving no trail to follow back down. The climbers descended in a whiteout, so they could see few landmarks to guide them. They were living a nightmare, the classic recipe for disaster on K2.

Even the self-possessed Viesturs actually thought to himself, "We are going to die up here," as dread turned to near panic. He focused harder, channeling the adrenaline rush of fear to sharpen his senses. The ghastly descent was made worse by small slab avalanches that fell from above, and a gnawing doubt that they were going in the wrong direction. It started snowing harder. Viesturs took the lead. "We were just feeling our way down," he remembers of those desperate hours, "looking for something familiar. Finally we came to a gully I recognized from the way up—and I knew we were on the right route." They eventually found the tents of the high camp, but even then their troubles weren't over. New Zealand climber Gary Ball had become incapacitated by altitude sickness there, and Viesturs and Fischer, along with Mace, had a dreadful time rescuing the climber in a full-on storm.

"Way too close," Viesturs says in retrospect. With a wife and two children, the forty-year-old climber is—and always has been—committed to climbing as safely as possible, given the inherent risks of venturing into the highest mountains on Earth. But the trip to K2 was memorable in other ways too.

"Going to Pakistan is totally different from going to Nepal," Viesturs says, "not just for the landscape, but the culture as well. Hiking up the rocky, desolate Baltoro Glacier is altogether different from being in the green and gentle landscape of Nepal, but the real impact in the Karakoram is the people and their religion. In Nepal, the locals are Hindus and

▲ Tibetan man with prayer wheel, Bouddhanath Stupa, Kathmandu ⌁ Nepal

◀ Gasherbrum Group, Karakoram Range ⌁ Pakistan

Buddhists, and they are more free and easy about other cultures. Pakistan is a Muslim country, and that demands more of the traveler, more effort to respect the stricter customs. But what you get in return can be worth the effort."

"The landscape, to a certain extent, dictates these differences," Viesturs continues. "For instance, in Nepal, when you reach a village, the porters just disappear into the village and take care of themselves. On the Baltoro, there are no villages, so the Balti porters, the men of the region who take part-time work to carry loads, need the basic stuff of life. Beforehand, you agree to provide the men who carry your gear with footwear, sunglasses, socks, a tarp, kerosene stoves to cook with, and flour, goats, and other food. You've got to provide them with all that food and fuel because you're going into a barren wilderness. If you're going to K2 and need fifty porters to get your gear in, that means you need about another fifteen porters to carry the food for the first fifty porters. You send porters back as their loads are consumed."

"The Balti porters are Muslim, so every day they kneel and pray, sometimes four or five times a day, depending on how devout they are, or what kinds of concessions they are making because of their jobs. It's fascinating. A few of them speak English, and that makes the interaction a lot easier. I honestly don't think the bond between most Western climbers and the Baltis is as close as the one that usually develops between Western climbers and some Sherpas. But the experience can be a moving one, and it's fun, at night when they're cooking up their chapatis (like flour tortillas), to sit around the fire with them,

share their food when it's offered, try to make a connection."

Part of what draws Viesturs to the Himalaya is his own unusual physiology. He has been subjected to laboratory studies that show he processes oxygen more quickly, better, and in bigger volumes than most of us. That and his high level of aerobic fitness allow him to excel at the kind of climbing he attempts. Like the handful of other climbers who make a mark on the biggest mountains on Earth, Viesturs has a rare talent, along with a psychological makeup that enables him to thrive on the challenge of pushing himself beyond the point of normal human endurance. On the eve of another trip to the Himalaya, during which he hopes to climb two 8,000-meter peaks in a single season, Viesturs can barely contain his excitement.

"I'm psyched," he says with unabashed enthusiasm. "I love going there. Compared to what's going on at home—getting ready, doing the speaking engagements, meeting the responsibilities we all have—it's just so busy at times that I can't help but be a little scattered. But when I go on an expedition, I can achieve total focus and simply absorb the tranquility of the landscape and the people around me. The hardest part for me is leaving my family and the day-to-day life I have with them. But when I do go on a climb, I have to focus totally on it, and that opens me up to the kind of experience I'm talking about. I have time during the day to sit and talk, to think. Get up in the morning and go to the next destination. Then, when I'm on the mountain, what I'm thinking about is 'Okay, we're climbing, this is why I'm here, this is what I do'."

▲▲ Paiju Peak (21,648 feet/6,598 meters), Karakoram
Range ᧞ Pakistan

▲ Buddhist monks blowing traditional horns, Tashi Samtenling
Monastery, Kathmandu ᧞ Nepal

▶ Woman, Lhasa ᧞ Tibet

▲ ▶ ▶▶ Kazakhs playing *buzkashi*, Pamir Plateau ⌔ China

▲ Porters, Baltoro Valley ⌁ Pakistan ▶ Biaho Lungpa River, Baltoro region ⌁ Pakistan

▲ Trango Tower region, Karakoram Range ⌒ Pakistan   ▶ Boulder, Biaho Lungpa River ⌒ Pakistan

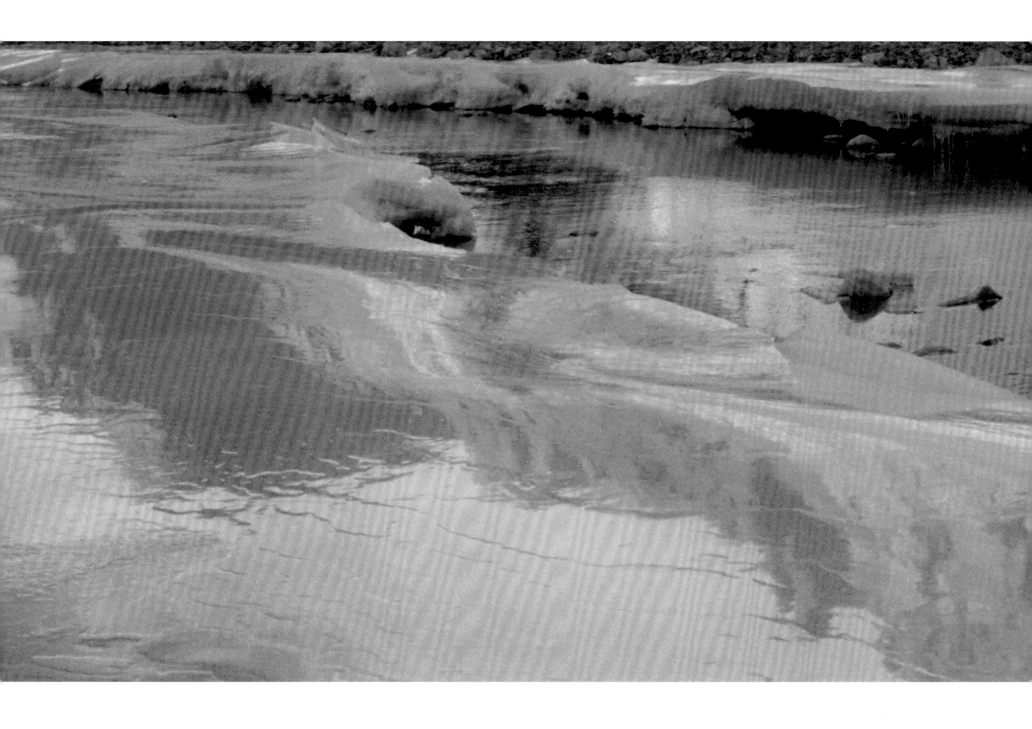

Rongbuk River ⌒ Tibet

▲ Mount Everest from the Rongbuk Valley ⌒ Tibet   ▲ Aerial over the Himalayan foothills ⌒ Nepal   77

Mount Everest from the Rongbuk Valley ⌇ Tibet

Star trails over Mount Everest ~ Tibet

▲ Prayer wheels, Bouddhanath Stupa, Kathmandu ❧ Nepal ▶ Woman praying, Lhasa ❧ Tibet

▲ Prayer flags, Bouddhanath Stupa, Kathmandu ❧ Nepal   ▶ Aerial over the upper Khumbu Valley ❧ Nepal

Concordia, Karakoram Range 〜 Pakistan

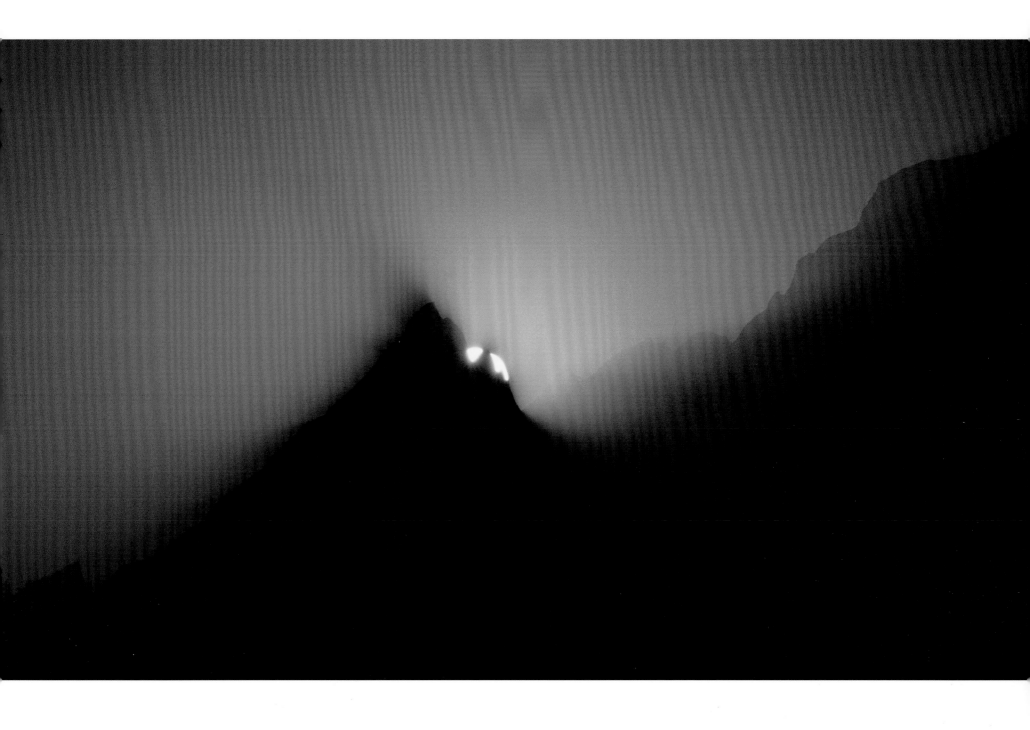

Sunrise above Baltoro Glacier ❧ Pakistan

Star trails, Karakoram Range ∽ Pakistan

Masherbrum (25,660 feet/7,821 meters),
Karakoram Range ∽ Pakistan

Broad Peak (26,400 feet/8,047 meters),
Karakoram Range ∼ Pakistan

Overlapping ridges, Karakoram Range ✌— Pakistan

▲   Seracs, East Rongbuk Glacier ✌ Tibet   ▶   Mitre Peak, Karakoram Range ✌ Pakistan

Buddhist monks, Tashi Samtenling Monastery,
Kathmandu ∽ Nepal

Potala Palace, Lhasa ∽ Tibet

▲ Machapuchare (22,956 feet/6,997 meters),
Annapurna Himal ⌢— Nepal

Great Trango Tower (20,624 feet/6,286 meters),
Baltoro Muztagh Range ⌒ Pakistan

▲ Uli Biaho Spire, Baltoro Muztagh Range ᴧ– Pakistan   ▲ Trango Tower, Baltoro Muztagh Range ᴧ– Pakistan

Aerial view of the Khumbu region ❧ Nepal

Sunrise over Gasherbrum I, Karakoram Range ⌒ Pakistan

Reflecting pool, Baltoro Valley ᔕ Pakistan

Remote village, Pamir Plateau ⌒ China

Khumbu

▲ Steep summits above Pheriche ☙— Nepal

▲ Climbers and Ama Dablam (22,486 feet/6,854 meters),
Khumbu region ☙— Nepal

Muztagh Tower (23,882 feet/7,279 meters),
Karakoram Range ∼ Pakistan

◀ Lammergeier *(Gypaetus barbatus)* ✌ Tibet   ▲ Gasherbrum I, Karakoram Range ✌ Pakistan

Glacial lake and dwarf fireweed *(Epilobium latifolium)*,
Baltoro Glacier ∾ Pakistan

PHOTOGRAPHER'S FIELD NOTES

Pages 62–63, 68, 69, 70–71

Pamir Plateau, China
As I traveled toward Khunjerab Pass on the Chinese-Pakistani border, I saw an enormous cloud rising from the plain like a dust devil. To my delight it was a group of Kazakh men playing *buzkashi*, an ancient game of Central Asia. Literally translated as "goat grabbing," two teams play on horseback, each attempting to gain control of a headless goat.

All: Canon F-1, Canon FD 80–200mm lens, f/8 at 1/250 second, Fujichrome 100 film

Page 72

Baltoro Valley, Pakistan
Straining under heavy loads, porters endure icy, silty water rushing over hidden and unstable rocks. If a porter twists an ankle or strains a knee, he must return to his village without having earned expedition pay—pay critical to supporting his family.

Canon EOS-1N, Canon EF 17–30mm lens, f/8 at 1/250 second, Fujichrome Velvia film

Page 73

Baltoro region, Pakistan
A trekker looks out over the tumultuous rapids of the Biaho Lungpa River, swollen with meltwater off snowfields high above. Fast flowing and numbingly cold, these waters have claimed the lives of many people over the years.

Canon EOS-1N, Canon EF 70–200mm lens, Canon Extender EF 1.4x, f/16 at 1/250 second, Fujichrome Provia film

Page 74

Trango Tower region, Pakistan
After photographing a detail of the foreground rock in the Trango Tower using a macro lens, I decided to reframe the subject using a wide-angle lens. The resulting photograph juxtaposes the stratified rock and the granite spires beyond.

Canon EOS-1N, Canon EF 17–30mm lens, f/22 at 1/8 second, 2-stop graduated neutral density filter, Fujichrome Velvia film

Page 75

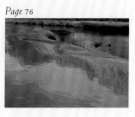

Biaho Lungpa River, Pakistan
The silt-laden rapids of the Biaho Lungpa River polish enormous boulders of stratified rock deposited by the receding Baltoro Glacier.

Canon EOS-1N, Canon EF 70–200mm lens, f/16 at 1/30 second, Fujichrome Velvia film

Page 76

Rongbuk River, Tibet
The most hazardous duty at Mount Everest's north base camp was getting water every morning from the nearby Rongbuk River. Negotiating the thick, slick ice along the river's edge while carrying two buckets of ice water was a chore that no expedition member wanted.

Nikon F3, Nikkor 20mm lens, f/22 at 1/15 second, 2-stop neutral density filter, Kodachrome 64 film

Page 77, left

Mount Everest, Tibet
A frozen puddle provides an interesting foreground for distant Mount Everest as seen from the banks of the Rongbuk River.

Nikon F3, Nikkor 20mm lens, f/22 at 1/15 second, polarizing filter, Kodachrome 64 film

Page 77, right

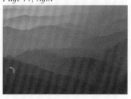

Himalayan foothills, Nepal
Morning mist helps distinguish one ridge from another in the foothills immediately south of the Khumbu region. The softness of the light, combined with the gentle slopes, creates a striking contrast to the glaciated mountains rising abruptly to the north.

Canon EOS-3, Canon EF 28–135mm IS lens, f/8 at 1/250 second, Fujichrome Provia film

Page 78, 79

Mount Everest, Tibet
Page 78: As winter gave way to spring, I discovered new opportunities to photograph Everest, here reflected in a pool of meltwater along the Rongbuk River. Page 79: Later I returned to the same spot to execute an 8-hour time exposure, capturing the arcing trails of stars across the sky.

Page 78: Nikon F3, Nikkor 20mm lens, f/22 at one second, polarizing filter, Kodachrome 64 film
Page 79: Nikon F3, Nikkor 20mm lens, f/4 at eight hours, Kodachrome 64 film

Page 80

Kathmandu, Nepal
Prayer wheels are an integral part of Buddhism, as they purify the mind. As you pass them on your right, the wheels are spun in a clockwise direction, as viewed from the top, so the characters on their faces can be read—and to travel in the same apparent direction as the sun. These are in the Bouddhanath Stupa.

Canon EOS-3, Canon EF 70–200mm lens, f/22 at 1 second, Fujichrome Velvia film

Page 81

Lhasa, Tibet
Buddhists spin prayer wheels as they chant a prayer. This woman was sitting with several other elders near the Potala Palace. All were pilgrims who had journeyed across Tibet to celebrate the Lunar New Year.

Nikon F3, Nikkor 80–200mm lens, f/4 at 1/60 second, Kodachrome 64 film

Page 82

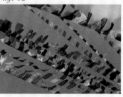

Kathmandu, Nepal
Strung upon lines attached to the top of the Bouddhanath Stupa, prayer flags inscribed with Buddhist prayers are attached to tree limbs and rooftops. Here, they provide a beautiful contrast to the large white structure. Using a polarizer, I deepened the blue sky, allowing the colorful flags to stand out.

Canon EOS-3, Canon EF 70–200mm lens, f/16 at 1/30 second, polarizing filter, Fujichrome Velvia film (pushed 1 stop)

Page 83

Page 84

Page 85

Page 86

Page 87

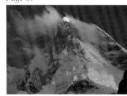

Page 88

Upper Khumbu Valley, Nepal
Flight affords an entirely new perspective of Nepal's upper Khumbu Valley. Ama Dablam rises in the center foreground, while Cho Oyu dominates the far ridge to the left. At 26,750 feet/8,153 meters, Cho Oyu is the sixth highest mountain in the world.

Canon EOS-3, Canon EF 28–35mm IS lens, f8 at 1/250 second, Fujichrome Provia film

Concordia, Pakistan
Expedition tents are raised at Concordia in the Karakoram Range. Here the mountaineer can see K2 for the first time along the Baltoro approach.

Canon EOS-1N, Canon EF 70–200mm lens, f/22 at 1/30 second, Fujichrome Velvia film

Baltoro Glacier, Pakistan
Suspended dust particles enhance another cloudless sunrise along the route to K2. After two weeks of sunny weather, a sudden rainstorm cleared the atmosphere above the Baltoro Glacier.

Canon EOS-1N, Canon EF 70–200mm lens, f/11 at 1/250 second, Fujichrome Velvia film

Karakoram Range, Pakistan
A jagged ridge above the Baltoro Glacier is silhouetted by the lingering light after sunset. To get this image, I first exposed for the light immediately above the ridge. I then exposed again with a 4-hour time exposure once the daylight had completely disappeared.

Canon EOS-1N, Canon EF 70–200mm lens, f/4 at 4 hours, Fujichrome 100 film

Masherbrum, Pakistan
The summit of Masherbrum in the Karakoram is fired with alpenglow. During the months of August and September, clear, stable weather sets in, providing climbers and trekkers alike with ample opportunity to experience this great range of jagged mountains.

Canon EOS-1N, Canon EF 70–200mm lens, Canon Extender EF 1.4x, f/11 at 1/8 second, polarizing filter, Fujichrome Velvia film

Broad Peak, Pakistan
Along with its immediate neighbors, K2 and the Gasherbrum Group, Broad Peak is one of the highest peaks of the famed Karakoram Range of Pakistan.

Canon EOS-1N, Canon EF 400mm lens, f/8 at 1/60 second, Fujichrome 100 film

Page 89

Page 90

Page 91

Page 92

Page 93

Page 94

Karakoram Range, Pakistan
I have always been drawn to monochromatic, backlit subjects. I love the way atmospheric elements such as fog, mist, and dust can transform the landscape into a translucent dreamscape.

Canon EOS-1N, Canon EF 70–200mm lens, f/16 at 1/30 second, Fujichrome Velvia film

East Rongbuk Glacier, Tibet
Like a colonnade of marching soldiers, seracs atop the Rongbuk Glacier in Tibet are carried down the valley.

Nikon F3, Nikkor 28mm lens, f/16 at 1/60 second, Kodachrome 64 film

Mitre Peak, Pakistan
Clouds swirl around the knife-edged summit of Mitre Peak high above Concordia. I have never been to a better location for photographing mountains than the Karakoram's Concordia. In every direction, a huge mountain is just waiting to be photographed.

Canon EOS-1N, Canon EF 70–200mm lens, Canon Extender EF 1.4x, f/11 at 1/250 second, polarizing filter, Fujichrome Provia film

Kathmandu, Nepal
Six Buddhist monks stand in silence within the walls of Tashi Samtenling Monastery. This is the second Samtenling Monastery; the first was located in Tibet and destroyed during the Chinese invasion of 1959.

Canon EOS-3, Canon EF 70–200mm lens, f/16 at 1/15 second, Fujichrome Provia film

Lhasa, Tibet
The Potala Palace shines in the afternoon sun. It is named after a sacred mountain in southern India regarded as the home of the bodhisattva Avalokitesvara. Tibetan Buddhists recognize the Dalai Lama as his reincarnation.

Nikon F3, Nikkor 80–200mm lens, f/13 at 1/30 second, Kodachrome 64 film

Mount Everest, Tibet
Prevailing winds stir up a billowing snow plume over Everest's Northeast Ridge, as viewed from Nepal.

Canon EOS-3, Canon EF 35–105mm IS lens, f/4 at 1/250 second, Fujichrome Velvia film

Page 95

Machapuchare, Nepal
Playfully called "Fish-tail Mountain," Machapuchare emerges from the clouds as they dissipate in the cooling temperatures of evening. The mountain makes a stunning backdrop for the city of Pokhara, Nepal.

Nikon F3, Nikkor 200–400mm lens, f/4 at 1/30 second, polarizing filter, Fujichrome 100 film

Pages 96, 97

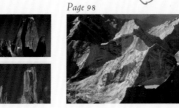

Trango Tower Group, Pakistan
The Trango Tower Group dominates the middle portion of the journey up the Baltoro Glacier to K2. The group's main components, Great Trango Tower, the Uli Biaho Spire and Trango Tower, are a challenge to the world's best rock climbers.

Page 96: f/16 at 1/15 second, polarizing filter
Page 97, left: f/11 at 1/60 second, polarizing filter
Page 97, right: Canon Extender EF 1.4x, f/11 at 1/30 second
All: Canon EOS-1N, Canon EF 70–200mm lens, Fujichrome Velvia film

Page 98

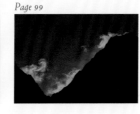

Khumbu region, Nepal
The heavily crevassed slopes of glaciers characterize the snowbound ramparts of the Khumbu region. A high concentration of 26,000-foot (8,000-meter) mountains makes it one of the two most spectacular regions of the entire Himalayan Range.

Canon EOS-3, Canon EF 28–135 IS lens, f/4 at 1/500 second, Fujichrome Provia film

Page 99

Gasherbrum I, Pakistan
Signaling the start of another brilliant day high in the heart of the Karakoram Range, the first rays of the rising sun set fire to the wispy clouds clinging to Gasherbrum I's lofty heights. To arrive at the proper exposure, I simply spot-metered off the highlighted clouds.

Canon EOS-1N, Canon EF 400mm lens, f/8 at 1/60 second, Fujichrome Velvia film

Page 100

Baltoro Valley, Pakistan
Stranded channels of the Biaho Lungpa River provide calm water for photographing reflections of the Karakoram Range. The terminus of the Baltoro Glacier can be seen below the lowest point along the horizon.

Canon EOS-1N, Canon EF 17–30mm lens, f/16 at 1/4 second, polarizing filter, 2-stop neutral density filter, Fujichrome Velvia film

Page 101

Pamir Plateau, China
In the treeless landscape, villagers gather the dung of their livestock for fuel. Once dried, dung burns hot—for cooking and for warmth.

Canon EOS-1N, Canon EF 70–200mm lens, f/16 at 1/30 second, Fujichrome 100 film

Page 102, left

Pheriche, Nepal
Often overlooked, the multitude of lesser-known summits of the Khumbu region above Pheriche would nevertheless be primary destination points in most other mountain ranges.

Nikon F3, Nikkor 200–400mm lens, f/11 at 1/30 second, polarizing filter, Fujichrome 100 film

Page 102, right ✳ ♡

Ama Dablam, Nepal
Two climbers on a small promontory survey the heavily fluted north face of Ama Dablam, one of the most highly sought summits in the entire high Himalaya. For this shot, I stood approximately 50 yards (46 meters) behind the climbers. Using a zoom telephoto lens at the 300mm focal length, I framed the climbers with the face of the mountain in front of them.

Nikon F3, Nikkor 200–400mm lens, f/16 at 1/8 second, polarizing filter, Fujichrome 100 film

Page 103

Muztagh Tower, Pakistan
Muztagh Tower straddles the border between Pakistan and China in the Karakoram. It offers one of the more rewarding views from the Baltoro Glacier. Using a wide-angle lens and a position near a rock with quartz bands, I composed my photograph so as to direct the viewer's attention toward the distant tower.

Canon EOS-1N, Canon EF 17–35mm lens, f/22 at 1/15 second, polarizing filter, Fujichrome Velvia film

Page 104

Lammergeier, Tibet
The 46-inch (1.2-meter) wingspan of the Lammergeier (*Gypaetus barbatus*) allows the vulture to soar high on thermals and live in mountain strongholds up to 25,500 feet (7,772 meters). Vultures are an integral part of the traditional Tibetan "sky burial," in which the dead are cut up and left exposed to the elements. It is believed that the birds complete life's cycle.

Canon EOS-1N, Canon EF 600mm, Canon Extender EF 2x, f/5.6 at 1/2 second, Fujichrome Provia film

Page 105

Gasherbrum I, Pakistan
Blocks of ice the size of buildings poke out of the surrounding rubble-strewn surface of the Baltoro Glacier. In the distance, Gasherbrum I and the rest of the peaks of the Karakoram's Gasherbrum Group rise high in the sky.

Canon EOS-1N, Canon EF 70–200mm lens, f/22 at 1/60 second, polarizing filter, Fujichrome Velvia film

Page 106

Baltoro Glacier, Pakistan
Dwarf fireweed (*Epliobium latifolium*) grows along the temporary shore of a small lake formed by a rockslide in the vicinity of the Baltoro Glacier. The pink color of the flowers was a welcome sight in a world of rock and ice.

Canon EOS-1N, Canon EF 17–35mm lens, f/22 at 1/15 second, 2-stop graduated neutral density filter, Fujichrome Velvia film

DOUG SCOTT

On the highest mountain on Earth, British climber Doug Scott found within himself the way to a life made remarkable by his embrace of the Himalaya. Scott experienced his epiphany—and, more incredibly, survived it—in 1975, on his third journey in three years to Mount Everest. He and Scotsman Dougal Haston made history on the world's highest peak at the dicey conclusion of their ordeal, which will be remembered forever by the title of the book it engendered: *Everest the Hard Way.*

The pair had reached the summit of Everest by the Southwest Face, a difficult and technical new route, but the climbers had reached the top too late in the day to descend, and had actually tarried there to enjoy the sunset view, which left them to face a deadly experiment. Haston and Scott would discover that night whether human beings could survive, intact, a bivouac at 28,700 feet (8,748 meters) without supplemental oxygen.

Inside their snow cave, the men rubbed their extremities, had conversations with imaginary partners, and drifted into a psychological netherworld of hypoxia. When dawn finally came, the two climbers were not only still alive, but virtually unscathed, a tribute to a sort of purity of purpose that Scott says comes only from total commitment. That day the exhausted men descended to the safety of high camps, and eventually to international acclaim. But Doug Scott's life would become increasingly influenced by the irresistible power of the Himalaya.

"That bivouac was crucial to me, a turning point in the

Photo © Greg Child

way I have lived," he confided one sunny February day in 2001 as we sat in a café on Maid Marion Way, in the shadow of England's Nottingham Castle. Though he now lives in the Lake District, farther north near Scotland, Nottingham was Scott's childhood home, and the nearby crags of Derbyshire his introduction to climbing and to life in the hills. We met there to talk over what it means to have spent the better part of forty years in the highest mountains on Earth, and with the people who live among them.

Now in his late fifties, Scott had just returned from Nepal, where he runs a trekking company with his Indian-born wife, Sharu, as well as a charitable trust to benefit the indigenous people of the Himalaya. The mountaineering achievements he made in that arena will endure along with Sir Edmund Hillary's, Reinhold Messner's, and a few others, but for Scott, the deepest rewards lie elsewhere.

The first of many journeys to the Himalaya began for Scott in 1967, but at the opposite end of the continent from Everest: the Hindu Kush of Afghanistan, near its border with Pakistan, a subrange lying at the extreme western end of the long, curving arc of Central Asian mountains. The next few years saw his first journeys to Everest, twice in 1972. Those were the beginnings of his strong connections to the people of the Himalaya. He had set off in search of extravagant challenge, and met that, but by accident he found a place and a culture that enriched his life in powerful, unexpected ways.

"Right from the start I found myself spending quite a lot

▲ Glacial lake, Baltoro Glacier ∾ Pakistan

◀◀ Terraced hillside, Pokhara ∾ Nepal

of time about the kitchen chatting with the Sherpas. You should always make friends with the cook," he says with a small laugh, "but for me there was something else than mere self-interest: the sense that I could learn something from these people. I was enjoying them, their way of life, and these places more with each trip, even if the Everest mountaineering tactics still amounted to a siege."

Climbing expeditions to Everest and other 8,000-meter peaks in the 1960s and '70s had such huge teams and appalling amounts of equipment because of the decision to take oxygen. "In those days," Scott says, "the bottles weighed 16 pounds (7 kilograms) each, and it was obviously necessary to have lots of people to get the stuff in position, along with all the fixed rope." The style of climbing made any expedition to the mountains a cumbersome affair.

"That's why what happened in 1975 is so important," he said. "It occurred to me after the bivouac on Everest that if I could spend the night out at the top without oxygen, then I could obviously risk spending a night out anywhere. It really opened up a world of opportunity, it widened the range of what I might do next and, more importantly, how I might do it. I knew I could go much lighter, much less expensively—and therefore more frequently.

"Going to the Himalaya in that sort of lightweight style meant it could be less time-consuming in terms of organization, with small teams, just friends, really, and few sponsors. I could go twice a year, and generally move quickly and quietly through the countryside to the climb. You just walk, you go there. That's how you get to know the people, and the place."

In the next twenty-five years, Scott traveled from one end of the great Asian range to the other, from Everest in eastern Nepal to K2 in the Karakoram of Pakistan; from Kanchenjunga in northern India to Shishapangma in Tibet; to Nuptse, Broad Peak, Makalu, India's Changabang and Shivling, Nepal's Baruntse, and a dozen other regions. In the course of doing some of the most challenging mountaineer-

ing in history in a bold and committed lightweight style, a funny thing was happening to Scott.

"I began to notice that my interest in going to the Himalaya was as much to be back with the people and the mountains as it was to climb," he says with a look of matter-of-fact wonder at that long-ago revelation. "It's hard to know what it is about those people in the Himalaya that results in such a strong effect on others, but it's easy to see the result."

Scott's exposure to the landscape and cultures of the Himalaya was so immersive that its effect on him was perhaps inevitable. But what amazes him is that the same sort of transformation happens to almost everyone who goes there, and it happens immediately.

"I like to look through the feedback questionnaires that the trekkers from our co-op fill in," he says, smiling. "Many of these people are total neophytes, and even if they've gone out in the mountains for just a week, they all come back saying, 'It's changed my life.' I think what they're really saying is that their contact with the people has changed them.

"The wonder," he emphasizes, "is how these people, among the poorest in the world, with so little in the way of amenities, so little material prosperity, without so much as running water or piped gas, can be so happy. And not just happy and content with themselves, but warm and welcoming to strangers. In the interaction between the cultures, it's we Westerners who become changed. Here in the West, we've got everything, and yet generally when our time in the mountains is over, we come back to more stress and discomfort than these people ever seem to feel. In some ways we come back to lives that are out of our control, in total contrast to the people of the Himalaya.

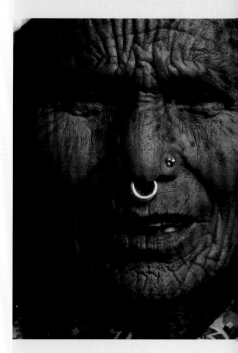

"What strikes me most strongly," he continues, "is the fact that they live their life at a very tranquil rate, seem to know exactly who they are, and don't want to be anything they aren't. My friends among these people are well centered, they are balanced with themselves. I can tell you that has a quite singular effect on me. Just being in their presence calms me right down.

And when I come back home, they remain in my mind, and their lifestyle remains in my mind as a good reference point of just where we might be—or perhaps aspire to be."

Given the obvious dangers inherent in high-altitude mountaineering, it was perhaps inevitable that the close friendships Scott developed with Himalayan people would at times turn tragic. In his account of a 1987 climb on the Northeast Ridge of Everest, Scott described the sudden loss of his friend Nima Tamang, who was buried in a freak avalanche on the usually safe yak trail into the Rongbuk base camp on the north (Tibetan) side of the mountain. Nima had been on Scott's expeditions to the Himalaya for most of a decade, and had visited his home in England. For Scott, the unexpected avalanche—on the heels of a historic snowfall—was a great shock resulting in a deep personal loss.

"Nima was the only person I know who seemed to be in perfect harmony with himself and the world," said Scott. "When I was leaving our advance base camp to attempt the mountain, I had suggested to Nima that he use my sleeping mat. He said, 'That would be very nice, Sahib, but when you come back you will need it, and, having got used to it, I will miss it, so I'd rather not bother.' We learned more from Nima than he ever did from us."

Scott has spent more time with the Sherpas of Nepal than with other mountain people, but he knows many cultures. Scott's forays to remote regions and exotic cultures began in the mid-1960s, when he found his way to the Cilo Dag mountains of Turkey. He was moved by his contact with the locals, struck by hospitality and generosity of spirit shown to him by the Kurdish nomads who visited his base camp. Scott shakes his head, remembering, and says that he only hopes they have survived the recent political turmoil that has wracked their homeland.

His relentless search for climbing objectives he might attempt in his preferred style—lightweight, multinational, and in the company of friends—took Scott to the remote corners of the Himalaya. Frequent trips to K2 and other peaks in the Karakoram such as Broad Peak offered rich opportunity for Scott to spend time with the Baltis, the people who live in the region of the great Baltoro Glacier. "Some people find the Baltis more difficult than people from cultures such as the Sherpas," he said, "but when the chips are down you see how tough yet compassionate these people can be."

Scott would know. In 1977 he faced one of the most desperate times of his long climbing career. Having reached the summit of the daunting and dramatic Ogre in the central Karakoram's Latok group, Scott broke both legs on his first rappel from the top. What was already going to be a difficult technical descent became a problematic struggle for life with an uncertain outcome. Despite the near-hopeless situation, Scott was able to descend to base camp, mostly under his own steam, crawling and dragging himself along during an eight-day ordeal that has since become legendary. But even at base camp, Scott's troubles weren't over. He was a long way from help, and his only hope was the Balti porters.

"When I broke my legs on the Ogre," remembers Scott, "eight of the porters came up as a stretcher party to carry me down the Biafo Glacier. It was a painful experience, but a wonderful way to learn about these people. For days I listened to them chatting away, listened to them decide which route to take, when to take a rest, make camp, go out to get wood, make a fire, cook dinner. All of it was done with nothing more than a low babble of conversation. There was no obvious leader, and yet everyone knew what had to be done and just did it. And all this time they were thinking of me and looking out for me. I just thought that that's how great expeditions ought to run.

"I think that one of the main reasons the hill people have our affection," he says, "and the reason they have balance and contentment, is because they bring their kids up in a way in which the child is never doubtful of who he is. What I've noticed over the years is how really good these people are with children, anyone who is disabled, anyone who is suffering or has had an accident, as I did in Pakistan.

▲ Grand Cathedral (19,045 feet/5,866 meters), Baltoro Muztagh Range ∽ Pakistan

◀ Rural home, Khumbu region ∽ Nepal

They seem to naturally reach out to help in a way that is disarming.

"At night, in the houses of my Sherpa friends in Nepal, I've seen the Sherpas up on the (sleeping) bench; there's mom and dad with baby in between, next oldest, and so on, maybe the grandparents at the far end. When a child wakes up in the night and reaches over, there's somebody he recognizes instantly, there's absolutely no distance, and any worries just evaporate. During the day he's been carried in the field or bounced around on someone's back on the way to market, but he was never out of arm's reach of some member of his family. That's just totally opposite to the way we live here in the West, with mom and dad rushing off to work, leaving kids in some child-care place, everyone sleeping in separate rooms, the kids alone with their fears.

"In the Himalayas, every time the kids need attention, it's given; they never have to seek it, they never have to wonder who they are. Because they are brought up in contentment, they remain so."

Scott sees parallels between the Balti and Sherpa peoples, and the dozens of other mountain cultures he has come to know, a common thread he argues might come from the be-

ginnings of our own humanity. After an arduous adventure with the Nishi people of the remote mountains of eastern India's Arunachal Pradesh, Scott was impressed with the individuals of this hunter-gatherer society.

"It struck me then that this was how probably all our ancestors were. Arguably for two hundred thousand years we've been recognizably human, and here's perhaps the last remnant of how all our ancestors were. Was it survival of the fittest, or survival of the most social? Is it possible that we are inherently good, innately cooperative, and these people still show it? I think so, and I think all people of the Himalayas show varying degrees of that.

"For us, all that has become hidden under the layers of our Western society, behind our comforts. An interesting question is raised just by being among these people: how and why have we turned our backs on our humanity and basic spirituality? Sometimes I wonder if perhaps we have to go through these trappings of what we think of as modern life, the desire for greater comfort and security, in order to come back to where we started. The Himalayan people can show us how we might have been, perhaps how we were meant to be, deep down, and how we might be again."

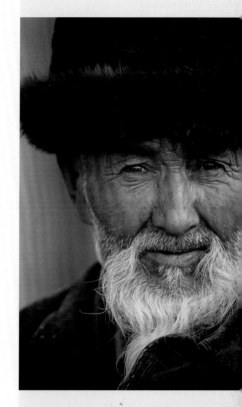

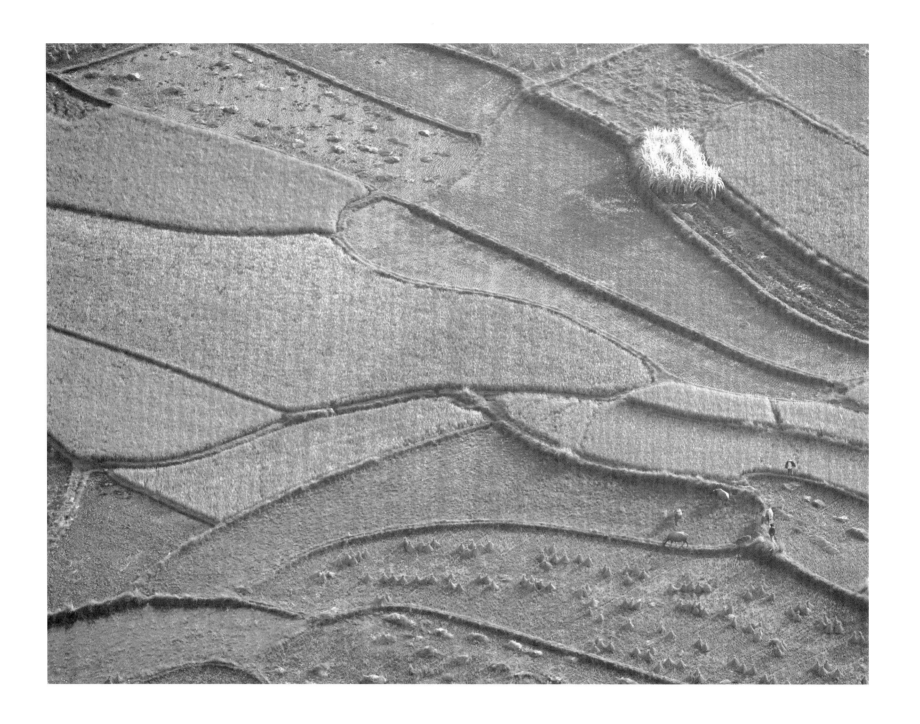

▲ ▶ Cultivated fields, Askole village ～ Pakistan

▲ Star trails over Thamserkhu ∽ Nepal

▶ Gasherbrum Group, Karakoram Range ∽ Pakistan

◀ Wall mural, Rongbuk Monastery ✐— Tibet　　　　▲ Tibetan youth, Lhasa ✐— Tibet

Unnamed Peak, Khumbu region ∾ Nepal

Ridge between Nuptse and Lhotse Shar,
Khumbu region ॐ Nepal

123

Light and shadows, Pamir Plateau ∽ China

Lower slopes of Mount Kongur (25,326 feet/7,719 meters),
Pamir Plateau ~ China

▲ ▶ Yak train, Rongbuk Valley ∿ Tibet

◀ Petroglyphs, Hunza Valley ᨀ Pakistan ▲ Siberian ibex *(Capra ibex sibirica)*, Karakoram Range ᨀ Pakistan

◀ Terraced fields, Hunza Valley ᾱ Pakistan   ▲ Rock wall, Hunza Valley ᾱ Pakistan   131

Gentian *(Gentiana spp.)*, Baltoro region ∾ Pakistan

Rooftop, Namche Bazaar ∼ Nepal

▲   Lesser panda *(Ailurus fulgens)*, eastern forests,
Himalaya ⌇ Nepal

▶   Forest interior ⌇ Nepal

Mixed forest near Thyangboche Monastery ～ Nepal

▲ Prayer flags and homes, Namche Bazaar ◇— Nepal   ▲ Porters, Khumbu Valley ◇— Nepal   137

▲ Naga sadhus, Varanasi, Uttar Pradesh State ⁓ India

▶ Floating candles on the Ganges River, Varanasi, Uttar Pradesh State ⁓ India

◀ Pasu Peak (23,899 feet/7,284 meters),
Hunza Valley ∼ Pakistan

▲ Herders en route to wintering grounds,
Pamir Plateau ∼ China

141

▲ Broad Peak and Gasherbrum Group from
Concordia ～ Pakistan

▶ Pheriche, Khumbu Valley ～ Nepal

Mount Everest and Middle Rongbuk Glacier ∾ Tibet

Rock on ice pedestal, Baltoro Glacier ♪ Pakistan

▲ K2, Karakoram Range ᳇ Pakistan

▶ Expedition climber at Camp III (21,000 feet/6,468 meters),
Northeast Ridge, Mount Everest ᳇ Nepal

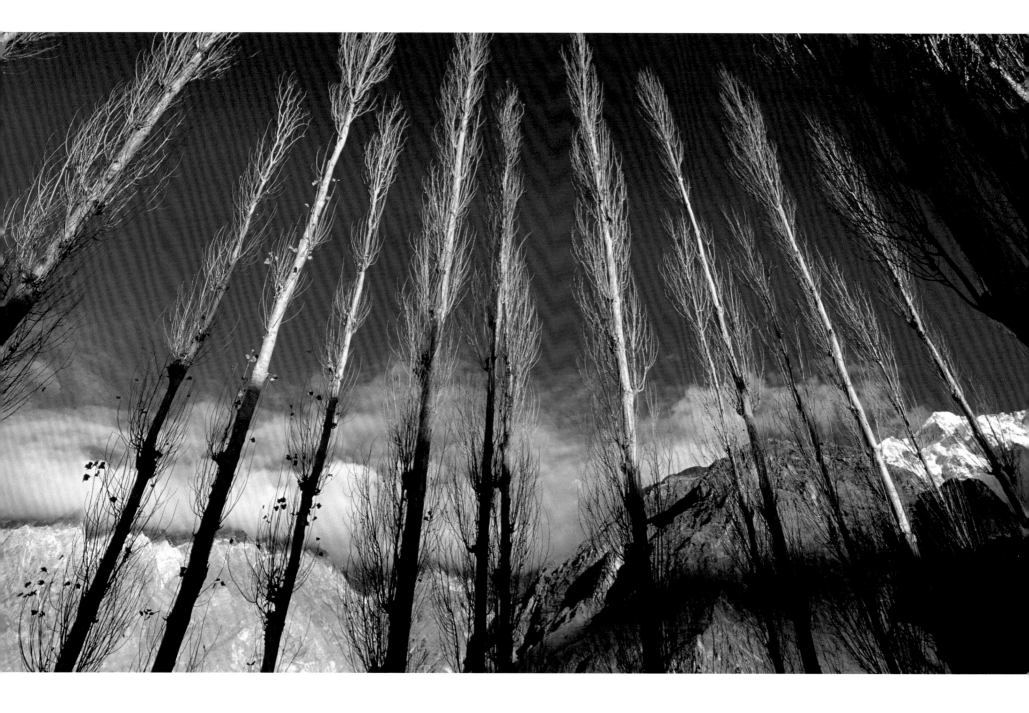

Himalayan poplar trees *(Populus ciliata)*,
Hunza Valley ∾ Pakistan

▲ Icicles along Rongbuk Glacier ∿ Tibet

▲ Baltit Fort, Hunza Valley ∿ Pakistan

149

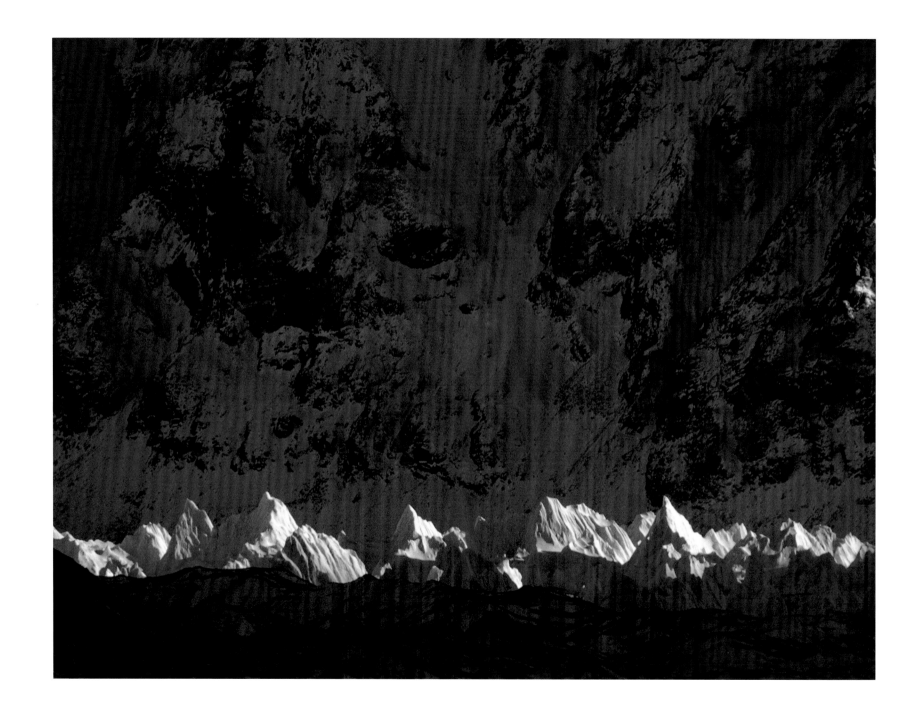

Khumbu Glacier ⌇ Nepal

Snow leopard *(Panthera uncia)* ‿ Himalaya Range

Sadhu babas, Varanasi, Uttar Pradesh State ❧ India

▲ Naga baba, Varanasi, Uttar Pradesh State ⌒ India

▶▶ Purification ceremony along the Ganges, Varanasi,
Uttar Pradesh State ⌒ India

153

PHOTOGRAPHER'S FIELD NOTES

Pages 110–111

Pokhara, Nepal

In a mountainous country like Nepal, flat, farmable land is scarce. Villagers utilize as much of the steep hillsides as possible by terracing the land. On the hillsides above Pokhara, extensive networks of rice terraces dominate the landscape.

Nikon F3, Nikkor 400mm lens, f/16 at 1/15 second, Fujichrome 100 film

Pages 116, 117

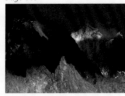

Askole village, Pakistan

Askole is a small town along the main expedition route to the K2 region. Its location in the valley along the Biaho Lungpa River makes farming ideal. Wheat, corn, and rice are grown in broad terraces.

Canon EOS-1N, Canon EF 70–200mm lens, f/16 at 1/30 second, Fujichrome Velvia film

Page 118

Thamserkhu, Nepal

From the vantage point of Namche Bazaar, the two peaks of Thamserkhu appear as twin summits. To get this shot, I took two exposures on the same slide. First, I exposed for the sun's afterglow on the peak. Then, as night fell, I re-exposed for the stars, taking an 8-hour time exposure.

Nikon F3, Nikkor 200–400mm lens, peaks—f/4 at 2 minutes, stars—f/4 at 8 hours, Fujichrome 50 film

Page 119

Gasherbrum Group, Pakistan

Late-afternoon light highlights the overlapping ridges of the Gasherbrum Group as viewed from Concordia in the Karakoram.

Canon EOS-1N, Canon EF 70–200mm lens, Canon Extender EF 1.4x, f/16 at 1/15 second, Fujichrome Velvia film

Page 120

Rongbuk Monastery, Tibet

When the Chinese invaded Tibet in October 1950, they destroyed many of Tibet's remote monasteries, including this one in the Rongbuk Valley. While visiting in 1984, I crawled through the rubble and discovered a hidden chamber. With a flash mounted to my camera, I was able to illuminate this mural.

Nikon F3, Nikkor 28mm lens, f/11 at 1/60 second, flash, Kodachrome 64 film

Page 121

Lhasa, Tibet

Wearing a hat of sheep's wool, a young Tibetan boy confidently stares into my lens. When I passed through Lhasa in the winter of 1984, very few Westerners had been permitted to visit Tibet. We were treated as a great curiosity.

Nikon F3, Nikkor 80–200mm lens, f/8 at 1/125 second, Kodachrome 64 film

Page 122

Unnamed Peak, Nepal

In the Khumbu region, Unnamed Peak glows in the last rays of the setting sun. The dramatic angle of the sun across the peak's face highlights the numerous "snow flutes" created by frequent avalanches.

Nikon F3, Nikkor 200–400mm lens, f/11 at 1/60, polarizing filter, Fujichrome 100 film

Page 123

Khumbu region, Nepal

A steep, south-facing ridge 22,727 feet (7,000 meters) high runs between Nuptse and Lhotse Shar. The ridge is too sheer to accumulate much snow. Several vertical glaciers begin at its base, however.

Nikon F3, Nikkor 200–400mm lens, f/8 at 1/125 second, Fujichrome 100 film

Page 124, 125

Pamir Plateau, China
Page 124: The 15,000-foot (4,572-meter) Pamir Plateau climbs into the north slope of the Himalaya.
Mount Kongur, China
Page 125: A yak herd grazes along a lake at the base of Mount Kongur. At 25,326 feet (7,719 meters), Mount Kongur dominates the landscape southwest of Kashgar on the Pamir Plateau.

Both: Nikon F3, Nikkor 200–400mm lens, Fujichrome 100 film
Page 124: f/16 at 1/60 second
Page 125: f/16 at 1/8 second

Pages 126, 127

Rongbuk Valley, Tibet

Both: On our 1984 Everest expedition to the Northeast Ridge we used yaks instead of porters to carry supplies to 21,000-foot (6,468-meter) Camp III. Surefooted and tough enough to endure snowstorms, yaks are the perfect choice in such rugged terrain. The sounds of their bells often precede their arrival.

Nikon F3, Nikkor 400mm lens, f/4 at 1/125 second, Kodachrome 64 film

Page 128

Hunza Valley, Pakistan

For European traders, the Hunza Valley was the main route through the Himalayan Range and into Eastern Asia. This was the famed "Marco Polo route." But long before Westerners arrived, people were using the valley as a primary path through the difficult range. These ancient petroglyphs depicting ibex are proof of this.

Nikon F3, Nikkor 80–200mm lens, f/16 at 1/8 second, Fujichrome 100 film

Page 129

Siberian ibex, Pakistan

In the Karakoram, a large male Siberian ibex (*Capra ibex sibirica*) scans the terrain ahead. Ibex are one of the primary prey of the snow leopard (*Panthera uncia*). Consequently, they are always very cautious.

Canon EOS-1N, Canon EF 600mm, Canon Extender EF 1.4x, f/11 at 1/30 second, Fujichrome Provia film

Page 130, 131

Hunza Valley, Pakistan
Page 130: The effortless geometric patterns first attracted my attention to the terraces of these Hunza Valley potato fields.
Page 131: A wall of carefully wedged stones is remarkably stable. In a landscape with little available wood, villagers become adept at using stone.

Page 130: Nikon F3, Nikkor 80–200mm lens, f/11 at 1/60 second
Page 131: Nikon F3, Nikkor 200–400mm lens, f/22 at 1/30 second,
Both: Fujichrome 100 film

Page 132

Gentian, Pakistan
Wildflowers like these gentian (*Gentiana spp.*) grow amid the protective shelter of a boulder-strewn slope above the Baltoro Glacier. If not for the protection of rocks, the drying winds would quickly kill any plant.

Canon EOS-1N, Canon EF 100mm Macro lens, f/22 at 1/8 second, Fujichrome Velvia film

Page 133

Namche Bazaar, Nepal
Taking full advantage of the infrequent precipitation during the dry season, farmers plant crops such as lettuce and cabbage close to their eaves in Namche Bazaar. When a summer shower does fall, the rain is gathered by the roof and directed onto the plants.

Nikon F3, Nikkor 80–200mm lens, f/16 at 1/15 second, Fujichrome 100 film

Page 134

Lesser panda, Nepal
Lesser pandas (*Ailurus fulgens*) inhabit steep slopes, thickly forested with bamboo, rhododendron, and oak. They eat primarily bamboo, but also roots, berries, insects, and rodents. Because of their specialized diet, low reproduction rate, and low population density, lesser pandas are extremely vulnerable to changes in the environment. (captive)

Canon EOS-1N, Canon EF 600mm lens, f/5.6 at 1/60 second, Fujichrome Velvia film

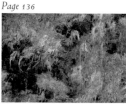

Page 135

Forest interior, Nepal
Deforestation, primarily from logging and agriculture, has devastated much of the dense forests that once blanketed the southern, midaltitude slopes of the Himalaya. Fortunately, a few parks and preserves have been established to protect some of the remaining forests of India, Nepal, and Bhutan.

Canon EOS-3, Canon EF 70–200mm lens, f/22 at 1/8 second, Fujichrome Velvia film

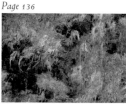

Page 136

Mixed forest, Nepal
Beautiful moss- and lichen-shrouded forests of rhododendron, birch, and evergreens surround Nepal's Thyangboche Monastery. At 13,000 feet (4,004 meters), the forests were an unexpected surprise and provided a contrast to the surrounding ramparts of rock, ice, and snow.

Nikon F3, Nikkor 200–400mm lens, f/16 at 1/30, Fujichrome 100 film

Page 137, left

Namche Bazaar, Nepal
Located in a steep, horseshoe-shaped basin, Namche Bazaar is the largest settlement en route to Mount Everest's south side. The homes are built on terraces. As the prayer flags attached to rooftops slowly disintegrate, the prayers are scattered to the heavens.

Nikon F3, Nikkor 80–200mm lens, f/16 at 1/15 second, Fujichrome 100 film

Page 137, right

Khumbu Valley, Nepal
Porters follow the well-worn route up the Khumbu Valley toward Nepal's Mount Everest base camp. The route is both scenic and strenuous as it traverses steep cliffs, following the rugged relief of this spectacular valley.

Nikon F3, Nikkor 200–400mm lens, f/8 at 1/125 second, Fujichrome 100 film

Page 138, 139

Varanasi, India
Sadhus, Hindu holy men, mass in Varanasi's narrow streets. Every twelve years some 3,000 make a pilgrimage to participate in the Khumb Mela, the world's largest gathering of sadhus. It is an honor to set a lighted candle adrift on the holy waters of the Ganges, which originate high in the Himalaya.

Page 138: Canon EOS-3, Canon EF 70–200mm zoom, f/11 at 1/60 second, Fujichrome Provia film (pushed 1 stop)
Page 139: Canon EOS-3, Canon EF 17–35mm lens, f/11 at 1/15 second, Fujichrome Provia film

Page 140

Pasu Peak, Pakistan
Showing the effects of a long dry season, Pasu Peak's lower slopes are clear of snow, while only its summit is shrouded in clouds. Soon snow will begin to accumulate as the monsoon season arrives.

Nikon F3, Nikkor 20mm lens, f/22 at 1/8 second, 2-stop graduated neutral density filter, Fujichrome Velvia film

Page 141

Pamir Plateau, China
Having spent the summer months in the high mountain valleys, herders bring their goats, sheep, and yaks down the mountains ahead of winter's onslaught. A donkey and a camel transport the rest of their personal belongings.

Canon EOS-1N, Canon EF 70–200mm lens, f/11 at 1/125 second, Fujichrome 100 film

Page 142

Broad Peak and Gasherbrum Group, Pakistan
We established our high camp at Concordia in the Karakoram amid the boulders in the foreground—all of which rest atop the slow-moving Baltoro Glacier. At night, as we lay in our sleeping bags, unnerving sounds of grinding ice serenaded us.

Canon EOS-3, Canon EF 17–35mm lens, f/22 at 1/15 second, polarizing filter, 2-stop graduated neutral density filter, Fujichrome Velvia film

Page 143

Pheriche, Nepal
An unusual white yak stands in a small pasture in Pheriche. In the distance, the upper Khumbu Valley awaits as we make our way up the valley. Pheriche is the last small town en route to Mount Everest along the Khumbu route. Drying yak dung is wedged in between the rocks, allowing it to dry as fuel, but also keeping the fence from blowing over. Wood is very scarce.

Nikon F3, Nikkor 20mm lens, f/16 at 1/15 second, Fujichrome 100 film

Page 144

Rongbuk Glacier, Tibet
Trailing a snow plume generated by constant high winds, Mount Everest looms over the Rongbuk Glacier. The extremely broken surface of the glacier would be all but impossible to traverse but for the medial moraine that permits access to the Everest's Northeast Ridge.

Nikon F3, Nikkor 50mm lens, f/16 at 1/8 second, polarizing filter, Kodachrome 64 film

Page 145

Baltoro Glacier, Pakistan
An interesting phenomenon occurs with rocks being carried by the Baltoro Glacier. Summer temperatures often soar over 100 degrees Fahrenheit (38 degrees Celsius). Boulders large enough to create significant shade become suspended when the surrounding ice not in the shade melts away over time.

Canon EOS-1N, Canon EF 17mm–35mm lens, f/22 at 1/30 second, Fujichrome Velvia film

Page 146

K2, Pakistan
The summit of K2 reflects the first light of a new day. Called Chagori by the local Baltis, many would argue that K2 is more spectacular than Mount Everest. A clear photograph of K2's summit was my primary objective during a monthlong trek through the Karakoram Range.

Canon EOS-1N, Canon EF 70–200mm lens, Canon Extender EF 1.4x, f/8 at 1/15 second, polarizing filter, Fujichrome Velvia film

Page 147

Mount Everest, Nepal
A high-altitude climber checks out his oxygen bottle at 21,000 feet (6,468 meters) at Camp III on Everest. In the days to come, he will use the oxygen as needed as he ascends the Northeast Ridge toward the summit.

Nikon F3, Nikkor 16mm lens, f/8 at 1/125 second, Kodachrome 64 film

Page 148

Himalayan poplar, Pakistan
At first glance, Himalayan poplar trees appear far too fragile to withstand the brutal weather so often associated with the Himalaya. In reality, their flexibility permits these trees to yield to the high winds without snapping. These are in Pakistan's Hunza Valley.

Canon EOS-1N, Canon EF 17–35mm lens, f/22 at 1/8 second, polarizing filter, Fujichrome Velvia film

Page 149, left

Rongbuk Glacier, Tibet
As I explore new terrain, I am always on the lookout for subjects to photograph. By crawling beneath an overhanging wall of ice along the Rongbuk Glacier, I was able to incorporate these 7-foot-long icicles into my composition as intriguing foreground elements.

Nikon F3, Nikkor 20mm lens, f/16 at 1/15 second, Kodachrome 64 film

Page 149, right

Hunza Valley, Pakistan
Baltit Fort, once home to the royal Mir family of the Hunza, is seen at the bottom of this photograph. Hunza Kunji (25,543 feet/7,786 meters) dominates the horizon near Karimabad, Pakistan.

Nikon F3, Nikkor 80–200mm lens, f/22 at 1/15 second, Fujichrome Velvia film

Page 150

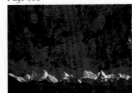

Khumbu Glacier, Nepal
The heavily fractured surface of the Khumbu Glacier is illuminated by a shaft of light passing between steep mountain slopes. The Khumbu Glacier's icefall immediately above base camp is considered the most dangerous portion of the climb up the West Ridge of Mount Everest.

Nikon F3, Nikkor 200–400mm lens, f/16 at 1/30 second, Fujichrome 100 film

Page 151

Snow leopard, Himalaya
In summer the snow leopard is found up to 19,686 feet (6,000 meters) in Central Asia's mountains. In winter it follows its wild and domestic prey down into the forests. Like the tiger, the snow leopard is hunted for both its fur and bone, which is used in some traditional Asian medicines. Consequently, they are highly endangered. (captive)

Canon EOS-1N, Canon EF 70–200mm lens, f/11 at 1/250 second, Fujichrome Velvia film

Page 152, left and right

Varanasi, India
Both: These sadhus have made a pilgrimage from the Ganges's headwaters in the Gangatri Glacier of the Garwhal Himal to participate in the Khumb Mela. Every twelve years, sadhus from all over India and Nepal gather to bathe at the confluence of the Ganges and the Jumna. These two sadhus prefer to wear their hair in tight coils; the sadhu pictured at left has not cut his hair in forty-eight years.

Canon EO-3, Canon EF 70–200mm lens, f/11 at 1/125 second, Fujichrome Provia film

Pages 153, 154

Varanasi, India
Page 153: A Naga baba or "naked wise man" sits in front of a fire attended by younger sadhus. He has lived a life of deprivation, shunning worldly goods.
Page 154: After a bath, a sadhu returns water to the Ganges—a ritual repeated thousands of times each morning as Hindus arrive at the sacred river.

Page 153: f/16 at 1/15 second, Fujichrome Provia film
Page 154: f/16 at 1/30 second, 2-stop graduated neutral density filter, Fujichrome Velvia film
Both: Canon EOS-3, Canon EF 17–35mm lens

157

SELECTED REFERENCES

Boardman, Peter. "Sacred Summits: A Climber's Year." In *The Boardman Tasker Omnibus.* Seattle: The Mountaineers Books, 1995.

Bonington, Chris. *Annapurna South Face.* New York: McGraw-Hill, 1971.

———. *Everest: The Hard Way.* London: Hodder and Stoughton, 1976.

———. *Everest Years: A Climber's Life.* London: Hodder and Stoughton, 1986.

Curran, Jim. *K2: Triumph and Tragedy.* Boston: Houghton Mifflin, 1987.

Craig, Robert. *Storm and Sorrow in the High Pamirs.* New York: Simon and Schuster, 1980.

Diemburger, Kurt. "The Endless Knot: Mountain of Dreams and Fate." In *The Kurt Diemburger Omnibus.* Seattle: The Mountaineers Books, 1998.

Gillman, Peter, ed. *Everest: Eighty Years of Triumph and Tragedy.* Seattle: The Mountaineers Books, 2001.

Herzog, Maurice. *Annapurna.* New York: Lyons and Burford, 1997.

Hornbein, Tom. *Everest: The West Ridge.* Seattle: The Mountaineers Books, 1998.

Houston, Charles. *K2: The Savage Mountain.* Seattle: The Mountaineers Books, 1979.

Mariani, Franco. *Where Four Worlds Meet: Hindu Kush, 1959.* Translated by Peter Green. New York: Harcourt Brace, 1964.

———. *Karakoram: The Ascent of Gasherbrum IV.* London: Hultchinson, 1959.

Matthiessen, Peter. *The Snow Leopard.* New York: Penguin Nature Classics, 1978.

Merriam-Webster, Inc. *Merriam Webster's Geographical Dictionary.* 3d ed. Springfield, Mass.: Merriam-Webster, 1998.

Messner, Reinhold. *Everest: Expedition to the Ultimate.* Seattle: The Mountaineers Books, 1999.

———. *The Crystal Horizon.* Seattle: The Mountaineers Books, 1998.

———. *To the Top of the World: Challenges in the Himalaya and the Karakoram.* Seattle: The Mountaineers Books, 1992.

Rowell, Galen, and Ed Reading. *Many People Come Looking, Looking.* Seattle: The Mountaineers Books, 1980.

Roskelley, John. *Nanda Devi: The Tragic Expedition.* Seattle: The Mountaineers Books, 2000.

Shipton, Eric. "Blank on the Map." In *Eric Shipton: The Six Mountain Travel Books.* Seattle: The Mountaineers Books, 1997.

———. "Mountains of Tartary." In *Eric Shipton: The Six Mountain Travel Books.* Seattle: The Mountaineers Books, 1997.

———. *That Untravelled World.* London: Hodder and Stoughton, 1969.

Joe Tasker. "Savage Arena." In *The Boardman Tasker Omnibus.* Seattle: The Mountaineers Books, 1995.

Tilman, H. W. *The Seven Mountain Travel Books.* Seattle: The Mountaineers Books, 1997.

RESOURCES

The American Himalayan Foundation
900 Montgomery Street, Suite 400
San Francisco, CA 94133 USA
Phone: (415) 288-7245
Fax: (415) 434-3130
ahf@himalayan-foundation.org
www.himalayan-foundation.org

Central Asia Institute
617 South Fifth Avenue
Bozeman, MT 59715 USA
Phone: (877) 585-7841 (toll-free)
Fax: (406) 586-9516
info@ikat.org
www.ikat.org

Community Action Nepal
Chapel House
Low Cotehill
Carlisle, Cumbria CA4 OEL UK
Phone: 01228 562358
Fax: 01228 562368
trekstc@aol.com

International Snow Leopard Trust
4649 Sunnyside Avenue North, Suite 325
Seattle, WA 98103 USA
Phone: (206) 632-2421
Fax: (206) 632-3967
info@snowleopard.org
www.snowleopard.org

Wildlife Conservation Society
2300 Southern Boulevard
Bronx, NY 10460 USA
Phone: (718) 220-5100
Fax: (718) 364-4275
feedback@wcs.org
www.wcs.org

INDEX References to photographs are printed in bold type.

ART WOLFE

Art Wolfe is one of the most highly acclaimed and widely published nature photographers of our time. A native Seattleite, he travels nearly nine months of the year on a personal mission to document the natural world on film. His honors include a 2000 Alfred Eisenstaedt Award for Magazine Photography, the 1998 Nature Photographer of the Year Award from his peers, and also in 1998 the first-ever Rachel Carson Award from the National Audubon Society for his work in support of the national wildlife refuge system. He has released forty-five books to date, including *The Living Wild, Water, Rainforests of the World, Tribes, Migrations*, and *Light on the Land*.

REINHOLD MESSNER

Reinhold Messner is widely recognized as one of history's greatest Himalayan mountaineers, a man who pushed back the frontiers of the possible for an entire generation of climbers. He was the first person to climb all fourteen of the world's 8,000-meter peaks, the first person to climb Mount Everest without oxygen, and the first person to solo Mount Everest. Messner is the author of more than a dozen books on climbing and the Himalaya, including *Free Spirit* and *Crystal Horizon*. Elected to the European Parliament in 1999, he has become an advocate of wilderness protection. His latest book focuses on his interaction with mountain cultures all over the world.

PETER POTTERFIELD

Journalist Peter Potterfield writes about wilderness travel and mountaineering for newspapers, magazines, books, and online publishing. He served as editor and publisher of *MountainZone.com* from 1996 to 2000, pioneering live reporting of Everest expeditions and other real-time mountaineering events from remote locations. Potterfield has made a specialty of covering mountaineering and wilderness adventure for the popular press, and he has written on these subjects for *Outside, Reader's Digest, Summit, Backpacker, Conde Nast Traveler*, and other national publications. He is the author of four books on the subject, including the critically acclaimed *In the Zone* (The Mountaineers Books, 1996).

ED VIESTURS

Ed Viesturs is poised to become the first American climber to reach the summit of all the world's 8,000-meter peaks, having climbed thirteen of the fourteen without supplemental oxygen by spring 2001. Viesturs became America's best known high-altitude climber when he appeared in the IMAX film, *Everest*, based on the eventful 1996 spring season there, and the NOVA film *Into the Death Zone*. During both film projects, he climbed Everest on cue. Viesturs's feats of high-altitude climbing include his ascent of both Manaslu and Dhaulagiri on a single expedition in spring 1999, during which he climbed Dhaulagiri alpine-style in three days.

NORBU TENZING NORGAY

Norbu Tenzing Norgay is Director of Development of the American Himalayan Foundation, a San Francisco based not-for-profit organization that provides humanitarian assistance to the Himalayan region. The son of world-renowned climber Tenzing Norgay, who with Edmund Hillary was first to the summit of Mount Everest in 1953, Norbu comes from a family of accomplished climbers, which includes ten members who have summitted Everest. Born and raised in Darjeeling, India, Norbu attended the University of New Hampshire where he received a Bachelor of Arts degree. He has traveled extensively around the world, particularly in his native Himalaya.

DOUG SCOTT

Doug Scott's historic ascent with Dougal Haston of the Southwest Face of Everest in 1975 marked a turning point in the way climbers approached Himalayan peaks. From then on, Scott led the way toward climbing the world's highest peaks in lightweight style, without oxygen. He soon completed major climbs on Shishapangma, Shivling, Nuptse, and Kanchenjunga, where his ascent of the North Ridge with Pete Boardman and Joe Tasker ranks among the great Himalayan climbs. He continues to climb in the Himalaya, where he operates a trekking business and a charitable trust to benefit the people of the Himalayan region. He is the author of *Himalayan Climber* and other books.

Aerial view of Kangchenjunga (28,169 feet/8,586 meters) on the right and Makula (27,824 feet/8,481 meters) in the left foreground ⌒ Nepal